WIN
EVERY
BATTLE

WIN EVERY BATTLE

Michael Galiga

BRONZE BOW  PUBLISHING

All Scripture quotations, unless otherwise indicated, are taken from the *Holy Bible, New International Version*®. NIV®. Copyright © 1973, 1978, 1984 by International Bible Society. Used by permission of Zondervan Publishing House. All rights reserved.

Scriptures noted NASB are taken from the *New American Standard Bible*®. Copyright © 1960, 1962, 1963, 1968, 1971, 1972, 1973, 1975, 1977, 1995 by the Lockman Foundation. Used by permission.

Scriptures noted NKJV are taken from the *New King James Version*. Copyright ©1979, 1980, 1982 by Thomas Nelson, Inc., Publishers.

Scriptures noted LB are taken from *The Living Bible*, copyright © 1971. Used by permission of Tyndale House Publishers, Inc., Wheaton, Illinois 60189. All rights reserved.

Scriptures noted from *The Message*. Copyright © 1993, 1994, 1995, 1996, 2000, 2001, 2002. Used by permission of NavPress Publishing Group.

Scriptures noted ASV are taken from the *American Standard Version* of the Bible.

ISBN-13: 978-1-932458-66-4; ISBN-10: 1-932458-66-2

Published by Bronze Bow Publishing, Inc.
2600 E. 26th Street,
Minneapolis, MN 55406

You can reach us on the Internet at www.bronzebowpublishing.com.

You can also reach us at www.wineverybattle.com.

Literary development and cover/interior design by Koechel Peterson & Associates, Inc., Minneapolis, Minnesota.

Manufactured in the United States of America

CONTENTS

IF

the corporate leaders

of any nationally recognized company,

which has no hope of survival apart from a

miracle, will agree to embrace and follow all

the concepts in this book, I will come and

lead them through the process.

That includes Chrysler, Ford,

General Motors, and Xerox.

What's the guarantee?

God will heal your business.

Michael L. Galiga

A COMMITMENT TO WIN

In May 1970, U.S. military intelligence received aerial photographs that revealed what was believed to be a POW camp near the town of Son Tay, some 23 miles west of North Vietnam's capital city. When American officials became convinced that 61 American POWs were being held there, they set in motion what many call the most daring military rescue operation of the Vietnam War.

At 2:18 a.m. on November 21, 1970, a joint group of 56 Army Green Berets volunteers and Air Force Special Operations Forces perfectly executed the raid, only to find the prisoners' quarters empty; the POWs had been moved to a different location. Having spent a total of 27 minutes on the ground, the raiders left behind 100–200 North Vietnamese casualties. American casualties for the raid were one wounded—a broken ankle.

Although the Son Tay Raid was a flawless success, it was a devastating disappointment to the men who risked their lives to carry it out. However, subsequent events proved that the audacity of the rescue attempt stunned the North Vietnamese. For their actions during the raid, the members of the task force were awarded six Distinguished Service Crosses, five Air Force Crosses, and 83 Silver Stars.

In his book, *You, the Warrior Leader*, Southern Baptist Convention President Bobby Welch writes that what many do not realize is there might not have been enough seats on the choppers to get all the POWs out. In this event, the 56 Green Berets committed to give their seats to the POWs and stay behind if necessary. The rescuers decided that if they needed to give up their seats, they would head to the bend in the Red River nearby and take up a fighting position.

This was their declaration: "Backed up to the Red River, we committed that we would fight until one of two things happened—someone came back to get us, or we died."

America needs millions of such men, and now they are assembling.

INTRODUCTION

Without a doubt, the key to winning every battle is aligning your life with the living God in the supernatural through a love relationship with God on steroids—no holds barred. Women seem to get this easier than men, but men have to discover this kind of relationship with the Lord. I suspect that there is a gene woven into each person's DNA that is designed to activate this indescribable love the moment we seek it.

Part of the reason I believe that is because of a little known scripture in Ecclesiastes 3:11 that says, "He has set eternity in the hearts of man, yet they cannot fathom what God has done from the beginning to end." What God has done from beginning to end is the greatest love story ever told, and He has woven it into the DNA of our hearts from conception. It is there ready to be awakened, dripping with love like the Song of Solomon describes in vivid detail.

The other reason I believe God's love is somehow woven into our hearts is because of my own experience. To grasp the situation, you must understand that I was not a child raised in church, and I'd been taught nothing about God. At the time, we lived in Phoenix, Arizona, where—for some reason—my mother started me in first grade when I was only five years old. I was the only five-year-old in the first grade at Alta Vista Elementary School. Yet even at that tender age, I had a great love for the Lord.

I may have reached out to Him earlier than some because of my circumstances. I was younger and smaller than all the other kids in my class, and in comparison, I felt so incredibly dumb. Each morning during my 20-minute walk to school, I talked to God, telling Him everything that was on my mind. During recess I played hard and simultaneously talked to God. I was fast and felt His pleasure when I ran. I talked to Him during my walk home. As much as was possible for a child, I worshipped God with every fiber of my being.

One day during first grade, I was playing marbles on a huge sidewalk with some other boys. My entire focus was on the cat-eye marble I'd just shot when everything around me went fuzzy. Today I would describe it as the feeling you get during anesthesia when the doctor tells you to count backward: 10...9...8...*fuzzy...nothing.*

Forty-seven years later, it is still hard to describe, but I went somewhere. I don't know where I went or what happened, only that the experience was good, powerful, and huge to a small boy. It felt as though I'd been gone for a long time when as suddenly as I'd gone, I was back watching my cat-eye marble. I looked around, shocked. I felt in some odd way as though I'd grown. I felt changed—older, stronger, wiser, and more focused. I looked at my buddies, certain that they could see the difference in me. I was stunned that they didn't seem to notice anything different. I felt sure they would cry, "What *happened?* Where did you *go?*"

They didn't ask those things and didn't seem to notice my absence. I had a sense that I'd been with God, although for what reason I had no idea. I felt complete peace about the experience. It was one of those moments forever captured in my memory. I can see the scene today as crisp and clear as it appeared to me then. I looked at my circle of friends and thought something that was years advanced beyond what I could have thought moments before: *I'm no better than them, but I'm different now.*

As an adult, I realize that was a weird thought for a five-year-old boy to have. Nonetheless, that's what I thought. In the days and months afterward, I continued talking to God and loving Him, though I don't recall being so scared or feeling so small. I never told anyone about the experience; how could I? It's hard to describe today. But about every six months afterward, I heard the Lord say, *"Mike, don't forget that day."*

"God, I could never, ever forget that day!" I answered, almost weeping.

For 47 years He reminded me to never forget that day.

It was a steamy summer day in July 2008, much like any other in Oklahoma, as I worked in my office. One moment everything was mundane; the next moment I felt overwhelmed by the manifest Presence of God in the room. I didn't have time to think, only react. One instant I was upright; the next instant I was prostrate on the floor, my arms outstretched. From somewhere deep within me, it felt as though words were being pushed out of my mouth.

"God," I cried, "if You don't tell me what You did in me that day when I was five, I'm going to die on this carpet right now!"

"Now you're ready, and so are they."

That doesn't sound like much of an answer, but I *knew* what He meant. He had placed a mantle of leadership on me when I was five. The message He put in me was now activated and ready to be delivered.

A few days later, I asked God, "Who are *they?"*

"Mike, it's everyone. The heavenlies have shifted. The battle has intensified exponentially, and there is no more middle ground—none."

I say the same thing to you today that I thought 47 years ago: I'm no better than anyone else, but my call is different than yours. Don't be mistaken; God has put eternity in your heart. His love is woven into your DNA, and He yearns for you to activate it. God has deposited things in you that only you can do. How do you get there? Through radical praise to God; by falling in love with Him.

The message that God gave to me is in your hands. It's a war cry from the heart of God: *You can win every battle! You must win every battle! It is time!*

1

SHIFTING INTO A NEW PARADIGM

I'm a businessman, not a pastor or an evangelist. I have a law degree and a degree in economics. While I don't have a Ph.D. in economics from Harvard, it doesn't take one to form an accurate assessment of our current economic crisis. In the simplest terms, if you were the economy, you would have been loaded onto an ambulance that screamed its way to the nearest trauma center. The emergency room doctors would have the paddles juiced up and ready to slam onto your chest in an attempt to revive you. It would be very questionable if you would be sent to the intensive care unit to recover or to the morgue.

Over a period of 60 days in late 2008, our national debt rocketed a jaw-dropping $8 trillion. Looking at a chart showing our debt history, you would see that around 1970 it started going up, and in 2000 it spiked almost straight up. If the chart was printed on standard 8 1/2 x 11 paper, when you added the $8 trillion of new debt, the line shooting upward would require seven or eight feet of paper to reach its current height. Worse, we can't pay back those loans. In addition, our banking system lost its liquidity almost overnight. Even with billions of dollars in federal bailout money, the banks aren't lending. They can't; they don't have the liquidity.

With the U.S. government crippled by debt, banks collapsing, and businesses failing, everyone seems to be asking for a piece of the pie. The line of businessmen outside of Congress looking for a handout is reminiscent of a soup kitchen during the Great Depression, except that many of the people in this line arrive in private jets.

The economic crisis in the United States is worsened by our global economy, which is so intertwined with other countries that when a Chinese merchant sneezes, a vendor in Lawrence, Kansas, catches cold. For example, the United States is the bread basket for the world. Grain grown primarily in Nebraska, Kansas, and Oklahoma is sent by rail to giant tanker ships, where it is distributed to other countries. In order for the grain to be taken off the train and put on the ship, there must be an irrevocable letter of credit, which is a promise from a major bank that if no one pays for the grain, eventually the bank will do so. Those transactions involve hundreds of billions of dollars, but when our banking system lost its liquidity, there were no letters of credit. If the problem isn't solved, eventually farmers could go bankrupt, and in time people in places such as Africa could starve.

> Most economists will tell you that our known resources are inadequate to fix these problems. The solution can only come from God's infinite supply.

In America today, many people are losing their homes to foreclosure, an increasing number of people have lost their jobs, and even more have lost some or all of their retirement. Gripped by fear, people worry about how to make their house payments, feed and educate their children, afford health insurance, and survive in their old age.

Most economists will tell you that our known resources are inadequate to fix these problems. The solution can only come from

God's infinite supply. The financial crisis has created a need for extraordinary help; for divine, supernatural intervention.

The reality is that life is filled with problems and challenges. Looking back over the past 100 years, we see that mankind has survived two world wars, the Holocaust, the rise of communism, and attempts at genocide against entire people groups. The economic crisis America faces today isn't the greatest problem we've ever faced, nor will it be the last. National and international problems aside, no one on earth is excluded from personal crisis, whether it comes in the form of financial problems, the pain of an abusive childhood, alcoholism that wrecks your life, children that get swept into a lifestyle of drugs, accidents, injuries, or disease—there are battles to be fought, and many of them seem overwhelming and impossible.

> National and international problems aside, no one on earth is excluded from personal crisis.

The shaking and quaking in our own lives and the world at large creates a crisis of faith. In troubled times, who can you trust? Where can you put your faith? How can you survive?

MY PERSONAL CRISIS

I am fortunate that I faced my own crisis years earlier. Mine was not a crisis of economy, but one that stemmed from my own soul and the questions that I needed answered. As a Christ follower and businessman, my crisis stemmed from what I read in the Bible. I read about a young shepherd boy turned king who won every battle he ever fought! In a time when every spring kings led their armies into war, that was no small feat. As a teenager, he killed a giant that had the entire army of Israel trembling in fear.

I read about a nation that, although they didn't win every battle, won every war and every single battle that God told them to fight. I read about a man who prayed that the sun would stand still so that there would be enough light for him to win his battle—*and it did.* I read about a man who lost everything—all his wealth, all his cattle, all his children, and all his friends. That man experienced total, overwhelming defeat; the kind of defeat from which no one can recover—*except he did.* God restored to him double for his trouble; double the money, double the flocks, double the herds, double the children, and double the favor. I read about a man who got rich during a famine. I read about a widow about to eat her last meal and die; instead, her oil never ran dry and she paid off all her debts and had money to spare.

> I dreamed of a day when God's supernatural power would attach itself to my business like rocket boosters.

The entire Bible is filled with stories about people who faced impossible odds and won every single time. Each time I read the Bible I wondered what it would be like to win every battle. I imagined what it would be like to have supernatural intervention in every part of my life. I dreamed of a day when God's supernatural power would attach itself to my own business like rocket boosters and give it more liftoff and thrust than the Space Shuttle, taking me to places I had never dared to go.

Each day after I read my Bible, I would close the book and take a hard look at my life. I had spent 32 years of my Christian life on the outside of the miraculous, longing for it, dreaming of it, but never able to experience it. The same three questions plagued me. *Where's the power? Where's the peace? Where's the wealth?*

FAST TRACK TO SUCCESS

Please don't misunderstand, by the world's standards my life was a picture of success. I knew from a young age that I wanted to work in commercial real estate. I was gifted in that area, and I sensed that it was my life's work, my destiny. After earning a degree in economics, I earned a law degree at Kansas University, taking every real estate course they offered. In May 1989, I went to work for Sam Walton, owner of Wal-Mart Stores, Inc. What I didn't learn about real estate in college and law school, I learned from Sam Walton, locating and purchasing prime commercial real estate. Sam and others took me under their wing and taught me things it had taken decades for them to learn.

During my first week with Wal-Mart, at an annual shareholders' meeting, an extremely wealthy real estate developer put his arm around me and gave me some advice. "Mike," he said, "you're young, ambitious, sharp, just out of law school, working for a fabulous company with a fabulous future ahead of you. But some day you're not going to want to do this anymore, and you'll need equity. You'll need to put deals together and own pieces of them."

I realized that he was telling me that at some point I would need to go into business for myself. With that advice tucked away for safekeeping, over the years I watched other people break away from a retailer with the idea of starting their own business and getting rich as a developer. In most cases, it was a slow, excruciating, painful, ugly death. Almost every one of them failed. So I started making mental lists of their mistakes. Year after year, I learned from those mistakes and determined not to make them when the time came for me to branch out on my own.

LIFE AT THE TOP

Meanwhile I was on a fast track to success, and it seemed as though everything I did turned to gold. I moved to California and developed commercial real estate for Target Corporation. In Milwaukee, I did the same thing for Kohl's Department stores as Director of Real Estate Development. For years I was senior vice president at General Growth Properties, the second largest retail real estate investment trust in the world and based in Chicago. We had a huge portfolio of our own, but we managed a $2 billion portfolio of non-owned properties. I had 52 clients worldwide—clients such as the United Bank of Switzerland, Citicorp, Cigna, the country of Abu

Dhabi, and many others too numerous to mention. I flew around the country making deals as part of the team that managed regional enclosed shopping malls, negotiating deals with Nordstrom's, Sax Fifth Avenue, Neiman Marcus, JC Penny's, Kohl's, Sears, Macy's, and everyone in between. I played with all the big boys and made a lot of money. I was living my dream.

At least I thought I did until I read my Bible. I had success, and I had money. But I was not experiencing the supernatural power of God. Although I can't deny that the hand of God and His favor were upon me, most of what happened during those years was driven by hard work. I worked hard, and when times got tough, I worked harder. When things got tougher still, I worked 15 times as hard. Even at the top of my game, I knew that there would come a day when I couldn't work that hard anymore. What bothered me most was that I didn't know how to tap into the supernatural power of God and see the miraculous in my life. I was successful by anyone's standards, but I lived in a constant state of stress and adrenalin rushes that took me from one deal to the next.

> What bothered me most was that I didn't know how to tap into the supernatural power of God and see the miraculous in my life.

FINDING GOD IN A NEW WAY

I didn't know how to win every battle—the battles of business, the battles of life, and the wars that bring you peace. I was at the pinnacle of success in my career, but as a Christian, I was on the outside looking in at what might have been. Thus began my journey to find God in a way I had never experienced Him. I knew the God who lay like a fictional character with one dimension on the pages of the Bible. I knew the God whom people worshipped from afar in their churches and synagogues.

I reached a point where I had to know Him as real, alive, reachable, and miraculous—or I was a dead man. Not dead physically, but dead to the miraculous that I knew swirled around me just beyond my grasp. I knew I *had* to go into the closet and meet with Him. That's when I threw myself face down on the floor and gave God all of me. It was there, face down in my closet, that the God of Abraham, Isaac, and Jacob—the Living God—met me. That's when I learned that I had stumbled onto the first great truth that will bring the miraculous into our lives. If God is going to give that much of Himself to us, He wants all of us in return—every cell and every atom.

> I had stumbled onto the first great truth that will bring the miraculous into our lives.

I wasn't the same man who pulled himself up off the floor that day. The man who walked out of my closet had tapped into the supernatural power of God. I knew without a doubt that my life would never be the same, and it hasn't been. From that day to this, I have seen the power of God go before me like He went before the Israelites and parted the Red Sea. I have stepped into such a relationship with God that I know beyond a doubt that *nothing* is impossible.

WINNING EVERY BATTLE IS NOT A FANTASY

Each of the following chapters includes true stories that help underscore what God has taught me about winning every battle. With the exception of my family, I've changed names and modified circumstances to protect the identities of those I have written about. As you'll see in this book, the principles that God has taught me have brought supernatural intervention to my personal life, my family, my business, and my finances. As I face the economic crisis ahead, I have not a single shred of fear. If we were to face a depression 50 times worse than the Great Depression following the stock market crash in 1929, I know that I would prosper and my family would never suffer lack. How can I know such a thing?

I have learned to win every battle.

Winning every battle isn't just a fantasy; it is a reality for me. And it can be a reality for each of you reading this book. You can do this too. Living in the supernatural is a lot like what athletes call being in the zone. Except the zone is unpredictable; the principles for winning every battle are 100 percent reliable and predictable. They work the same way in your personal life as they work in your corporate life. They work 24 hours a day, seven days a week, and 365 days a year.

> If we were to face a depression 50 times worse than the Great Depression following the stock market crash in 1929, I know that I would prosper and my family would never suffer lack.

If you will not just read but follow the principles in this book, you will experience God's supernatural intervention in your life. There's no problem too difficult for God. There's no company whose bottom line is too far in the red for God to restore. There's no government or economy on earth that can't be rescued by the power of God. What does such divine intervention require? It requires a complete, comprehensive paradigm shift. When you make that shift from living within the limitations of your own abilities and shift into the limitless power and resources of God, you will have tapped into a limitless supply of provision, miracles, and peace.

That's why I have issued this corporate challenge: If the corporate leaders of any nationally recognized company, which has no hope of survival apart from a miracle, will agree to embrace and follow all the principles in this book, I will come and lead them through the process. That includes Chrysler, Ford, General Motors, and Xerox. What's the guarantee? God will heal your business.

GOD'S LAWS AND MAN'S LAWS

I have a law degree, and I understand how the law works—but God's laws are higher than man's laws. To win every battle, you have to understand and tap into God's laws. That's what this book is all about.

I want you to understand that none of what has happened in my life is because I am special or even close to perfect. My feet are made of the same clay as yours, and I've made my share of mistakes. There is nothing you've ever done in your life that could disqualify you from experiencing God's supernatural power in your life. I don't care if you're reading this book from a prison cell or if you're living out your last days on Death Row. Once you know these principles and how they work, the only thing that will stop the supernatural power of God from manifesting in your life is if you read the principles but choose not to live them. God is a Gentleman, and He will never come into your life uninvited. Having said that, I don't think anyone in need of a miracle would make that mistake.

CORPORATE CHALLENGE

If the corporate leaders of any nationally recognized company, which has no hope of survival apart from a miracle, will agree to embrace and follow all the principles in this book, I will come and lead them through the process. That includes Chrysler, Ford, General Motors, and Xerox. What's the guarantee? God will heal your business.

There's no doubt about it—we are living in perilous times. But for those who tap into the supernatural power of God, this is the greatest time in the history of the world to be alive. You and I may never have to kill a giant named Goliath, but when we are faced with giant personal failures, giant debt, giant business failures, a government teetering on the edge of collapse, and a war against terrorism, we can tap into the miraculous.

We can—and will—win every battle.

2

SURRENDER BRINGS PEACE

W aves lapped against the sides of the USS Missouri, which sat anchored in Tokyo Bay on September 2, 1945, as a Japanese delegation headed by Premier Shigemitsu waited aboard a destroyer off the Missouri's bow. After boarding the Missouri, each of the Japanese saluted the American flag and the officer of the deck. General McArthur, Admiral Nimitz, and Admiral Halsey, along with delegates from Russia, China, the United Kingdom, Australia, Canada, France, the Netherlands, and New Zealand, greeted them on what has been dubbed the Surrender Deck. During the historic ceremony, gunmen manned the antiaircraft battery in the event that a kamikaze pilot attempted to crash the party.

General McArthur addressed the crowd and the ceremony opened with prayer. Soon after, officials from the Japanese government signed the Japanese Instrument of Surrender, officially ending World War II. Before the ink dried on the documents, the Imperial Japanese Navy ceased to exist and Japan readied itself for an Allied invasion. Although 50,000,000 people had died, Japan's surrender ended one of the bloodiest wars in the history of the world and brought great peace.

If you want to win every battle, the first and most important lesson you must learn is the power of Surrender. In business, you must be willing to surrender those things that have become unwieldy and obsolete and have the courage to face a changing economy with fresh vision for the future. In life, you must be willing to surrender your old paradigms for new ones. As in any war, you must know when to fight, and you must know when to surrender.

> To most of us, surrender is synonymous with defeat, not with victory.

I've got to be honest here and admit that for most Christians in the West the idea of surrender is as foreign as the concept of war. Yet that wasn't the case with the early Church; they knew evil existed and warred against it. How did the modern Church become so anemic and apathetic about spiritual warfare? In his excellent book, *God at War,* author Gregory A. Boyd explains that there are two different world views among Christians.

WARFARE WORLD VIEW

One of them is the Warfare World View, which is held by those of us who understand that the war in heaven, which began when Lucifer rebelled against God, is being played out right here on earth. Jesus said that Satan came to kill, steal, and destroy. The Bible also says that Jesus came to bring abundant life and to destroy the works of the devil. He knew we were in a war, and that's why He came to earth! *Because we understand this, we expect evil and are prepared to war against it. We aren't baffled by it.* Believers with this warfare world view know that they're in a war, but that they are working alongside God the Father, Jesus, and the Holy Spirit to enforce Satan's defeat.

Then there is the Classical Philosophical Christian World View in which people believe God is in total control and that He micro-manages the world. People with this world view are baffled by evil. *Why would God kill that child? Why would God send that tornado? Why did God let that Christian die of cancer?* The answer to all of those questions is some form of, "In order to teach us something." Those belief systems are not found anywhere in the Bible, but are born out of bewilderment over evil and the need to explain it in light of a loving God.

The classical world view puts all the blame for evil on God and lets both the devil and us get a pass. The truth is that the book of Genesis reveals that God created man and gave him dominion over all of the earth. When Satan took control by tempting Adam and Eve to sin, God sent Jesus to regain the authority that had been lost. Before He ascended to heaven, Jesus not only made sure the disciples understood that they were in a war, but He delegated His authority to them and through them to us, the Church.

He [Jesus] replied, "I saw Satan fall like lightning from heaven. I have given you authority to trample on snakes and scorpions and to overcome all the power of the enemy; nothing will harm you. However, do not rejoice that the spirits submit to you, but rejoice that your names are written in heaven."
LUKE 10:18–20

Why is this so important? If you believe that God is in the complete micromanaging control business, you'll misunderstand your role and responsibilities! Notice I did not say God was not in control; He is in control. He does, however, leave some things up to us. In order to win every battle, we must first understand that there is a war, and we play an indispensable part in God's war plan. We can change outcomes. We each have responsibilities and have much to say about how this battle goes. I admit it seems incomprehensible that the Living God leaves some things up to us, but He does. In order to win every battle, we must first understand there is a war and we are in it with a distinct role to play, like it or not.

HOW TO RESPOND TO EVIL SPIRITS

I read about a female reporter who interviewed a Marine Corps sniper. After a long interview, she finally asked the question she most wanted answered. "Imagine that you're in position with your loaded weapon sighted on the enemy," she said. "You're about to blow his head off. As you pull the trigger, what do you feel?"

"Recoil."

If you don't know, recoil is the kick of the gun as it's fired. That, I believe, should be our attitude about spiritual warfare. No fear, no regrets of vanquishing the enemy. Just recoil. I love this story.

Winning every battle requires total, unconditional surrender, not to our enemy—to God. When we surrender to the Living God, He prepares us for battle, and the Bible says that He covers us in the day of battle. We become His warriors to take back what the enemy has taken. IT is war, and we will not be baffled by evil. No fear.

I know that doesn't sound like a strategy that would make your business take a u-turn toward prosperity. It doesn't sound like the answer to the war that is raging within your own soul. To most of us, surrender is synonymous with defeat, not with victory. This is the first—and most important—shift in your paradigm. Total, unconditional surrender to God is the first—and most important—step toward total, unconditional success in every area of your life.

WINNING THE WAR IN BUSINESS

Often men call me who have crossed my path in business, seen me on television, or read about my work. The conversations all go something like this. "Hey, Mike. You don't know me, but I saw you on TV. I'm a businessman, and I'd like to buy you a cup of coffee. Fifteen minutes of your time is all I'm asking."

When we meet, he says, "I'm having problems with my business. I've got serious cash flow problems." I listen for an hour or more as he describes the battle he's facing in business. Once he's laid it out on the table, I respond.

"I think I understand the situation in your business, and there is a solution to the challenges you face, but fixing it is going to take more than 30 minutes or an hour. If you've got the time, I can give you my recommendations, and if you follow them, I think your cash flow problems will be resolved.

"Now that I understand the problem with your business, I need to explain something that you must know in order to turn your business around. You see, the invisible, supernatural world controls the natural world. The bottleneck in your business is a natural one, but those finances are being controlled in the invisible realm. In order to turn this situation around and win this battle, you've got to do more than just make natural changes. You've got to change things in the invisible realm. That's where most people miss getting their breakthrough. In the Bible, Jesus told us to pray for God's will to be done on earth as it is in heaven. What we need to do is pull heaven down to earth where your business is concerned.

> The invisible, supernatural world controls the natural world.

"In order to help, I need to know some things about you. First of all, I need to know where you stand with the Living God. You see, in my world view there are two kinds of people. The first group is people who have a relationship with the Living God. The other group are those who are about to have that experience. Which are you?"

THE GREAT EXCHANGE

Sometimes the person will say, "I've accepted Jesus, but I don't know how to bring heaven to earth." Other times the person may say, "I guess I'm in the group who is about to have that experience."

That's when I get to explain the greatest deal of the universe: Jesus takes all of our sins, defeats, failures, and problems, and in exchange He gives us the scepter of His authority to bring victory. The Bible gives us step-by-step instructions for the Great Exchange in Romans 10:9–11.

> *That if you confess with your mouth, "Jesus is Lord,"*
> *and believe in your heart that God raised him from the dead,*
> *you will be saved. For it is with your heart that you believe*
> *and are justified, and it is with your mouth that you confess*
> *and are saved. As the Scripture says, "Anyone who trusts*
> *in him will never be put to shame."*

This is a simple two-part process:

1. You believe in your heart (not just your head) that Jesus is the Son of God, and that God raised Him from the dead.
2. You confess with your mouth that you believe the above, and you confess that Jesus is Lord over your life.

This is the first and most important Surrender you'll ever make in your life. It's also the deal of a lifetime.

REMOVING THE CHOKEHOLD

"Look, Mike," you might say, "what does becoming a Christian have to do with stopping the hemorrhage in my business?"

That's an excellent question, and one I'm happy to answer. The first key to winning every battle is making sure you're on the winning team! As I explained earlier, this natural world, which includes your business and its bottom line, is controlled by the invisible, supernatural world. The invisible, supernatural world is divided into two parts. The first part is the Living God and the angels that make up His army. The other side is made up of Satan and the fallen angels who rebelled against God.

Jesus described Satan as a thief and said, "The thief comes only to steal and kill and destroy; I have come that they may have life, and have it to the full" (John 10:10).

WARFARE WORLDWIDE

I find the Bible very practical. Jesus said Satan is a thief, so in the invisible realm, who do you think has your business in a chokehold? You've got to switch things around in the invisible realm so that your business is ripped out of Satan's chokehold and put in position to receive God's supernatural intervention. Therefore, you have to choose sides, and nobody in their right mind would side with a thief.

> The first key to winning every battle is making sure you're on the winning team!

Suppose that your business and finances are in great shape, but you need to win the war over alcoholism or an addiction to drugs, pornography, or adultery. It doesn't matter what kind of war you're waging, the principles are all the same—and the first step is Surrender. You may need the chokehold removed from your mind, emotions, or your marriage. The first step is *always* Surrender.

MY FIRST SURRENDER

I was blessed to have good parents, but they didn't know the Lord. I never heard the Gospel message until I was 16 years old; until then I thought Jesus was a cuss word. At the time, Joe Wiley was an All-American running back for the University of Oklahoma, who maintained a four point average in accounting and later went on to play for the Oakland Raiders. Joe was among 12 football players, representing the Fellowship of Christian Athletes, who held an assembly at Putnam City High School in Oklahoma City. They were the embodiment of everything most of us wanted to become. That night a few of us got to meet Joe personally at a friend's house. Before the evening was over, Joe asked me a question that would change my life forever.

"Mike," he said, "have you ever asked Jesus into your life?"

"No," I admitted, "I haven't."

"Would you like to?"

I had never heard the Gospel message until that night, but for 16 years I'd looked for *something* that I knew was missing in my life. I wanted nothing more than to say yes and let Joe walk me through the process, but I was too embarrassed. "Let me think about it," I said.

Joe gave me a tract, and I left an hour later knowing exactly what I was going to do. I drove home, went inside, and ran up the stairs to my bedroom. Shutting the door, I fell on my knees and asked Christ into my life. I can't say that there was any lightning or thunderbolts, but I experienced a phenomenal clarity about what had just happened. I knew that I'd just made the most important decision of my life.

I believed that my eternity was secure.

It was the day-to-day life here on earth that tripped me up.

TEMPORARY SURRENDER

Don't get me wrong; from that day forward I saw divine intervention in my life. Jesus is the Door we each must go through to access both Father God and the Father's resources. There was no doubt that the Living God was involved in my life. I enjoyed a very successful career, but my life cycled in and out of spiritual highs and personal defeats. I didn't know how to break out of that cycle and win every battle. There are so many people who think that when you make Jesus the Lord of your life that you skip down the yellow brick road toward eternity without problems, or that there is no hope except hanging on until you die and awake with Jesus.

> I believed that my eternity was secure. It was the day-to-day life here on earth that tripped me up.

Nothing could be further from the truth. Christians face the same trials, tests, and tribulation that everyone faces in life. Our problem is that most of us never learn how to tap into the supernatural power of God that brings victory.

As you will see throughout this book, I did what most Christians do. I lived my life going from one temporary surrender to the next. I surrendered to the Lordship of Christ for eternity, but kept the reins of control over my day-to-day life. Whenever I faced a crisis and knew that I couldn't win, I cried out to God for help. God always intervened. When the crisis was resolved, I thanked the Lord and took back the control over my life until the next crisis.

> I lived my life going from one temporary surrender to the next.

It took me years to see that I was actually fighting God for control of my life. I was at war with the Living God.

I loved the Lord, but I identified with the apostle Paul who said that what he wanted to do, he didn't do; but what he didn't want to do he ended up doing! I kept tripping up and doing things I shouldn't have been doing. I kept going around the same old cycles of sin and defeat, and I had no idea how to break out of it.

A MAN GOD LOVED

God finally got my attention and began teaching me the principles in this book when I watched a documentary on television about King David, the second king of Israel. David started out as a shepherd guarding his father's flocks. He spent a good deal of time alone in the Judean hills where he wrote songs and sang in worship to God. The Bible says that David was a man after God's own heart. Yet, David committed adultery with Bathsheba, got her pregnant, and then ordered her husband murdered.

Adultery and murder? What was it that God loved about this man's heart?

It was that David had a personal, intimate relationship with God, and he was quick to repent. When a prophet confronted King David with his sin, David didn't justify himself or kill the prophet for speaking the truth. He had brought shame on himself, shame on Bathsheba, shame on his house, and shame on Israel. His sin had been found out.

I was riveted to the television as I watched the actor portray what David had done. Filled with sorrow, he threw himself face down onto the floor, arms outstretched, and repented. He wept, "God! Don't take Your Spirit from me! Please renew Your Spirit in me."

The king humbled himself before God, repented and turned away from his sin. God loved that humility so much that hundreds of years later, long after King David had died and been buried, the Bible says that God spared the city of Jerusalem simply because David had loved it. God had David's heart—all of it—every cell and molecule of his being.

No matter the odds, David always did whatever God asked him to do. This was very rare. The Lord also loved David's integrity. I realized that God desired no less from each of us.

TOTAL, UNCONDITIONAL SURRENDER

I knew right then what I'd been missing in my life. I got up off the sofa and went into our bedroom closet. I couldn't help thinking about all the people who need the encounter with the supernatural and are not free. I was going *into* my closet in order to die to myself and live for God. I knew before I ever stepped inside that what happened there would be massive. I shut the door and collapsed onto the floor where I lay face down with my arms outstretched before the Lord. I said, "God, I've been fighting against you for more than 30 years. You're infinite, and I'm finite—and I'm losing. You've been gracious to give me a wonderful family. You've been gracious to give me corporate jobs, promotions, and money. You've been gracious to give me a wonderful home.

"But there is incredible sorrow in my heart. So I'm here to settle this business with You. Of my own free will, I'm giving You every atom and every cell of my being. This decision is costing me every-thing. I'm giving you my wallet, my house, my family, my car, my busi-ness, my hopes, my fears, my past, my present, and all of my future."

After two hours, when I finally stepped out of that closet, I was not my own any more. There was a line drawn in the sand. I had sur-rendered everything to Him. Jesus was the Door whom I had walked through to become "As One" with the Living God. He was my God; I was His servant.

I didn't know what the future would hold, but I had the distinct impression that I had just embarked on the greatest adventure of my life. I couldn't help wondering what would happen.

THE POWER OF SURRENDER

Like David, I spent time each day praising God and fellowship-ping with Him. I was still new at the concept of total surrender when the Lord spoke one sentence that echoed throughout my heart.

"Mike, I want you to go to Israel."

To understand the significance of this, let me explain my situa-tion. For years I'd worked for major corporations, but I'd finally re-signed, moved home to Oklahoma, and started my own business. I was now in the same boat as many other successful businessmen I'd known over the years who left great benefits and job security to start their own business, only to watch it die a slow, agonizing death.

My business was young, and we were short on money. I don't mean that we didn't have groceries, we did, but financially we were in a hard place. My nature was such that when things got hard, I worked harder. If times got harder still, I worked 15 times as hard. When things get *really* tough, I work 1,000 times harder. Here I was in a hard financial situation and everything in me wanted to shift into high gear and work harder than I'd ever worked in my life.

What I *didn't* want to do was stop work, step away from the busi-ness, and go to Israel. That was diametrically opposed to my nature and my work ethic. However, I had surrendered every cell of myself to God, and that meant I was going to Israel.

"God," I replied, "I'll go to Israel as You have asked. I want You to know that I'll go to Israel whether You grant my requests or not. However, there are a couple of things that I need. First, we have two lots for sale in a development in Edmond. I would like to have both lots under a sales contract before I leave for Israel."

The response was instant.

"Okay...done."

"There's something else, Lord. I did a business deal with a guy named Keith from California. He owes me $200,000, and it appears that he isn't going to pay me. I want to be paid before I leave."

Once again, God's response was instantaneous.

"You go to Israel, and I'll take care of this."

LEARNING TO TRUST

This conversation occurred in February, and my trip to Israel was scheduled for June. Weeks and months passed but nothing happened. There wasn't a nibble of interest in the two lots we had for sale, and with each passing day it was clearer that Keith had no intention of paying me. However, I had fully surrendered to God, and I was going to Israel, so I spent time praising and worshipping Him each day. "God," I said, "I'm going to Israel no matter what. I'm going if the lots aren't under contract, and I'm going if Keith doesn't pay me. But I know those things will happen because You said they would, and You can't violate a promise to one of Your children."

A week and a half before I was scheduled to leave, our phone rang one night at 9:30 p.m. "Hey, Mike," the broker said, "I know it's late, but I got a great offer on one of your lots. Can I drop by?"

The offer was perfect, and we signed the contract that night.

One lot was now under contract, but nothing else happened. The night before I was scheduled to fly to Israel, I packed my bags and stacked them by the door in preparation for an early trip to the airport. I was getting ready for bed when the phone rang.

"Mike, I know it's late," the broker said, "but I got an offer on that other lot you have for sale. I'd like to bring it by tonight if you don't mind."

It was a perfect offer, exactly what we'd wanted, so we signed the contract that night. Both lots were now under contract, but not a hint of any money coming my way from Keith. I climbed into bed and said, "God, I've got a long trip to Tel Aviv and then on to Jerusalem, so I'm going to sleep tonight knowing that I'm in Your hands like I've never been before. I know that You cannot lie and You always keep Your promises. So I'm going to rest well."

> I imagined that this must be what a quarterback feels in a football game when there's 20 seconds left on the clock and he knows beyond all doubt that he's about to score a touchdown and win the Super Bowl.

THE ELEVENTH HOUR

I pulled myself out of bed at 4:30 the next morning and dressed for my journey. I'll admit that a part of me wanted to stay home and work, but I knew that was my old paradigm, so I shook it off. We arrived at Will Rogers World Airport where I said my good-byes to my wife and son before going through security.

I found a seat near my gate and watched the people around me reading newspapers, drinking coffee, and talking. I had an uncanny sense of embarking on a whole new chapter in my life. I knew that the Living God was about to do a miracle on my behalf, and the knowledge of it made the hairs rise on my arms. I imagined that this must be what a quarterback feels in a football game when there's 20 seconds left on the clock and he *knows* beyond all doubt that he's about to score a touchdown and win the Super Bowl.

My flight was announced, and I handed the attendant my boarding pass. Mine was a window seat, and there was nobody sitting beside me. I stowed my carry-on bag and buckled my seat belt as sun streamed through the window.

"God, this is the eleventh hour," I said.

The stewardess announced that the door would be closing in two minutes.

"God, that was the two-minute warning," I said. "I'm Yours, and I'm going to Israel no matter what. The rest is up to You."

I heard the door shut and felt the compression when it locked. The stewardess announced that all cell phones and electronic devices should have already been turned off. I pulled my cell phone out of my pocket, and a nanosecond before my finger pressed the OFF button...it rang.

The plane backed away from the terminal.

"Mike Galiga."

"Hi, Mike, it's Keith. Listen, I just wanted to let you know that we just made two $100,000 wire transfers into your account."

Seconds later, we ended our conversation. I turned off my cell phone and melted into my seat. *This was real.* The engines roared, the thrust propelling us upward where we soared toward heaven. *I hadn't done a thing to make this happen. I hadn't worked any harder. Yet the chokehold had been removed from my finances.* God was more real to me at that moment than the airplane that winged its way toward Israel. Riveted in my seat, in awe of God, I realized that there was no power on earth as great as the power of total Surrender to the Living God.

BATTLE PLAN

Japan's surrender to the Allies ended one of the bloodiest wars in the history of the world—and brought great peace. It doesn't matter what kind of war you're fighting, the first step to victory is always Surrender to the Living God.

BATTLE PRINCIPLES:

■ Surrender brings peace.

■ The invisible world controls the natural world.

■ The real battle will be won in the invisible realm.

■ You can't win if you're not on the winning team!

■ The Great Exchange activates the supernatural power of God on your behalf.

■ There is no power on earth greater than the power of total, unconditional Surrender to the Living God.

BATTLE STRATEGIES:

THE FIRST STEP: *The Great Exchange*
The first step to winning every battle is to make sure you're on the winning team. This is the First Surrender—and the greatest deal in the universe. By surrendering your life to Jesus, you surrender all your problems, faults, sins, and defeats; in exchange, Jesus grants you His strength, His righteousness, His power, and His authority.

The Bible explains the Great Exchange in Romans 10:9–11: That if you confess with your mouth, "Jesus is Lord," and believe in your heart that God raised him from the dead, you will be saved. For it is with your heart that you believe and are justified, and it is with your mouth that you confess and are saved. As the Scripture says, "Anyone who trusts in him will never be put to shame."

This is a simple three-part process:

1. You believe in your heart (not just your head) that Jesus is the Son of God, and that God raised Him from the dead.

2. You confess with your mouth that you believe the above, and you confess that Jesus is Lord over your life.

3. Jesus is the Door—walk through the Door into a relationship with the Living God, your Father, and into the abundance He provides.

Tell God about your problems. Confess your failures. Ask Jesus to be the Lord of your life. If you're not used to praying, don't freak out. It's just talking to God. Don't tell me you don't talk to anyone you can't see. We've all seen you do it in your car.

You're in a battle for your life. Don't wait. Don't move on to step two. *Do it now.*

THE SECOND STEP: *Total, Unconditional Surrender*
Now that you're on the winning team, you can do what I did and spend the next 30 years going from one temporary surrender to the next, but I don't recommend it. Temporary surrenders keep you on the outside of the miraculous, and let's face it, if you're going to win every battle, you need divine intervention. Besides, who wants to work harder and harder in your own finite power when God is willing to empower you to succeed with His unlimited power?

Tell everyone in your house that you need some time alone, even from the dog. You might as well turn off your cell phone. Shut the door to your bedroom. If your closet doesn't have carpet, you might want to put down a towel or blanket. I suggest you turn off the closet light and shut the door.

Now drop to the floor and lie face down. Tell God *everything.* I mean everything that is troubling you, everything that you regret, and all of your problems. Unload. Dump it all in His lap. Don't hold back—believe me, God can handle it.

Now, imagine that you're Japan and God is the Allies. Surrender. Everything. Surrender every atom and molecule of your being. Surrender all your hopes and dreams. Surrender your past, your present, and your future. Surrender your family and all those you love. Surrender every war you're attempting to battle. Surrender your business and your finances. Now ask Him to fight your wars and cause you to win every battle.

As you draw close to the Living God, He draws close to you. The supernatural now is invading the natural circumstances of your life.

"Wait a minute, Mike," you might say, "I'm going to be honest.... I'm *afraid* of God."

A lot of people are afraid of God, but it's only because they don't know Him. God isn't some distant tyrant who wants to get you. Listen, if God wanted to get you, you would have already been gotten! The Bible says that God created you. He formed you in your mother's womb. It says that God has a plan for your life—a plan for your good and not for your harm. Listen to this, the Bible says that God created you in His own image and He loves you so much that He *sings over you!*

God wants a personal relationship with you. So what if it's scary? That's where faith comes in. Take a deep breath and a step of faith into that closet.

Take this step before you go to the next chapter.

FORGIVENESS BRINGS FREEDOM

L ike most five-year-old children, Eddie's world revolved around his mother. She was his sun, the warmth that made him feel safe even after his father had died. He knew her scent, the way her hair smelled when she rocked him, and the soft feel of her arms around him that let him know he was protected and loved. He didn't know about the stock market crash or the Great Depression. He had no idea that they were poor or that other children had more food or toys. When his mother smiled at him, all was right with the world. When she hummed a tune, he knew that some day he would conquer the world. When she read him a bedtime story, he floated to sleep on dreams filled with peace.

"Eddie!" she called, the sound of her worn pumps clicking across the hardwood floor, signaling that it was time to go. Eddie skipped across the floor and slipped his hand inside hers. He chattered while she urged him into the bright yellow taxi. He snuggled close to her while she gave directions to the driver. Caught by the sights and sounds out the window, Eddie watched the changing scenery as though it were a movie.

The taxi pulled to a stop in front of a large house where Eddie skipped up the walk beside his mother. Inside, he followed his mother as she talked to people and looked around. When it was time to leave, Eddie heard her pumps clicking toward the door, and he raced to her side. When she stepped onto the gravel drive, strong arms grabbed Eddie and held him back. He fought, struggled, and screamed, *"Mommy!"*

Looking back, she said, "This is your new home. I can't afford to raise you. I have to leave." She climbed into the taxi and drove away.

Breaking free, Eddie chased the taxi down the gravel drive screaming, *"I hate you! I will never forgive you!"*

Eddie never saw his mother again. She never called. Though he waited and yearned for some contact, she never sent a letter, a postcard, or a gift on his birthday or Christmas. She never again acknowledged his existence. Every day that he didn't hear from her became a fresh stab of rejection.

Eddie grew up in the foster home where his mother left him and later became a CPA. When he was 45, he changed careers and prepared to enter the ministry. Something nagged at him, making him feel uneasy. After prayer, he sensed the Lord telling him that he should enter the ministry a whole person, not fragmented.

He had to deal with the pain of his past.

Eddie hired a private investigator to search for his mother. He tracked her down to a small town in Washington and handed Eddie her phone number. The voice that answered the telephone wasn't the voice of the young mother who hummed as she washed dishes. It was the voice of a little old lady who said, "Hello?"

"Mom, this is Eddie. I love you, and I forgive you."

For 40 years, Eddie had been stuck chasing that taxi down a gravel road. With those words he was finally free, finally whole.[1]

WHAT IS YOUR TAXI?

What taxi have you been chasing year after year?

Ten years later...30 years later...50 years later...you're still chasing that cab.

Don't kid yourself; we've all got our taxis—those old hurts and rejections that have been buried alive and are so deep that they've festered. You can't live in this world without getting wounded. I picture them a lot like the story of the giant in *Gulliver's Travels*. The giant lay on the ground while the little people threw ropes over him, only their ropes were nothing more than little strings to the giant. Hundreds of those little strings couldn't hold the giant; he could flick them off with his finger. But the little people didn't stop with hundreds; they threw thousands of the little strings over the giant. There were so many that when the giant tried to move, he was trapped. Even though he was hundreds of times more powerful, those strings mounted until they held him captive.

> Forgiveness is mandatory if you want to win every battle.

Imagine yourself as that giant. Every act of unforgiveness is a string.

Most of us have 50 by the time we're seven years old. By the time we're 10, we may have 100. By the time we're 20, we may have 1,000 of them. We think we can move and live our lives, but we're tethered by invisible bonds.

The only way to get free is to forgive.

FORGIVENESS IS THE HINGE

"Wait a minute, Mike," you might say, "you have no idea what they did to me."

You're right, I don't know. What I *do* know is that no matter what you do, if you ask God to forgive you, He forgives. Access to the Living

45

God hinges on forgiveness. The Bible says that if God is willing to forgive you for all your sins, you must be willing to forgive others. In the Lord's Prayer, we are told to pray, "Forgive us our trespasses as we forgive those who trespass against us."

The Bible makes it clear that if we want to be forgiven, we must forgive. In Matthew 18:23–35, Jesus told a parable about a king whose servant owed him a great deal of money. Since he couldn't repay the debt, the king ordered that he, his wife, and children be sold into slavery to pay it. The servant begged for mercy, and the king took pity on him and forgave the debt. Later, that same servant confronted a man who owed him a little bit of money. The man begged the servant for mercy, but he refused to give it to him. Instead, he had him thrown in prison. When the king heard what he had done, he was furious.

> Access to the Living God hinges on forgiveness

"You wicked servant," he said, "I canceled all that debt of yours because you begged me to. Shouldn't you have had mercy on your fellow servant just as I had on you?" In anger his master turned him over to the jailers to be tortured, until he should pay back all he owed. This is how my heavenly Father will treat each of you unless you forgive your brother from your heart" (vv. 32–35).

Forgiveness is mandatory if you want to win every battle. It's another layer of surrender, a process that we'll work through for the rest of our lives. You can't win every battle unless you're whole, and you will never be whole without forgiving.

A TWO-PART PROCESS

Forgiveness involves two components. The first is forgiving those who have hurt you, whether they meant to or not. You can do this on your own by getting a piece of paper and asking the Holy Spirit to reveal the source of both ancient and recent wounds, pains, rejections, and offenses; those that are small, and those that have grown deep roots of bitterness. Write them down, and then one by one, forgive each person involved and release them to God. Imagine a 55-gallon drum of sand, and you have a small tablespoon in your hand. That's how you begin emptying the barrel. Each time you give what's in your hand to God, more is removed from the barrel until one day it's empty—the pain is gone, and you are free. In the Bible, Jesus said to forgive 70 times 7, which equals 490. In Hebrew, that's the number for infinity. In other words, we are never to stop forgiving. Why? Unforgiveness locks us in the past and condemns the offender.

> The first part is forgiving others who hurt you; the second part is forgiving yourself.

Here's a tip drawn from wells of experience: The very toughest items of forgiveness require repetitive trips with the teaspoon to the 55-gallon drum of sand, perhaps even thousands. Then one day you're free. Be determined and faithful to keep going back to the barrel with the spoon. You'll feel it begin to lift and be replaced by freedom. A dark thing has been evicted, and light has taken its place.

The second component is often the toughest to do. You have to forgive yourself. That's huge, because the majority of those strings that have you bound were formed from your own hard judgments against yourself.

"But, Mike, I really messed up!"

I know, because we've all messed up, but when you repented of that sin, God forgave you. Now you must forgive yourself. Sit down with a piece of paper and ask the Lord to show you where you've hammered yourself through unforgiveness. With each layer of forgiveness, you will feel more light and free.

If you're fortunate enough to be near a deliverance ministry, I would encourage you to participate in it. I've been through two of them and found it very helpful. People in deliverance ministries are trained to help you get free of all those strings and help you be whole and healed of trauma. The first time I went through deliverance ministry was with

Everett Cox at City Church in Oklahoma City. Everett said, "Mike, have you ever been hurt?"

"Of course," I replied.

"Well, choose one of them," he said. "We'll get rid of it this minute. First, put your fist over your heart. Now think back to the pain, the person involved and how it felt. Put the whole event in your hand. Okay, now take a deep breath and lift it up to Jesus and say, 'Jesus, I give you this situation. You understand it; You experienced it. Take the pain from me now. I forgive this person and release them from my judgments.'"

I opened my fist and gave it to the Lord, and it felt like three pounds lifted off of me. Granted, it wasn't a lot of weight at first, but as I did this more and more often, I could tell a huge weight had been removed from me.

> First, He sees the blood of Jesus that was shed to take away your sin. The second thing He sees is all the things you've gotten *right*.

Forgiveness isn't something you do once and never do again. It's an ongoing process as we get wounds, bumps, and bruises in life. Even now I occasionally find myself driving down the street and remember something that happened 25 years ago. "Wow, Father, I'd forgotten about that," I say. "Thank you for bringing it to my memory. I forgive that person now. I take the pain and release it to You, the Living God."

FORGIVENESS IS SURRENDER

If your business partner, your spouse, your child, or friend hurts you, don't let it fester. Forgive and set yourself free to be healed. Once you've forgiven the people who hurt you, you've forgiven yourself and repented of your sins, when God looks at you, He sees two things. First, He sees the blood of Jesus that was shed to wash away your sin. The second thing He sees is all the things you've gotten *right*. Everything else, all your sins, mistakes, and failures are history once you repent. To God, it's as though they never existed. He looks at you and sees righteousness.

One reason many people resist forgiving is that they have the mistaken belief that forgiving someone means you condone what they did. That's not true. Forgiveness means that although you recognize what they did was wrong, you surrender the situation to God so that He will deal with it. You surrender your right to hold anger, bitterness, unforgiveness, judgments, and offenses.

> In the dark kingdom, there is a hierarchy of invisible, demonic spirits whose goal in life is to do whatever they can to wreck your life and your business.

Forgiveness is not reconciliation, because reconciliation requires two people. Forgiveness is an act you can do alone with the Living God.

Why must you let go of those feelings that, in many cases, are so justified?

Remember in the last chapter I told you that the unseen, invisible world controls the natural world? In the dark kingdom, there is a hierarchy of invisible, demonic spirits whose goal in life is to do whatever they can to destroy your life and your business. Because God is love, and because He offers forgiveness of all sins through His Son, it's clear that anger, bitterness, unforgiveness, judgments, and offenses come from the dark kingdom. God doesn't require you to forgive because He's hard or harsh; He requires forgiveness because unforgiveness, anger, bitterness, judgments, and offenses open spiritual doors through which demonic spirits can wreck havoc in your life.

God telling us to forgive is comparable to our warning our children, "Don't touch that!" when we see them about to get into something they don't recognize as deadly. We warn them out of love, and God does the same for us. That's the same reason He warns us not to sin. It's not because He can't or won't forgive us; it's because sin opens invisible pathways for demonic attacks.

Just because you can't see electricity doesn't mean it won't kill you if you stick a screwdriver into a hot outlet. The same is true of invisible, demonic spirits. There are critical spirits, spirits of unforgiveness, spirits of anger, and a whole host of other demonic spirits that are as real as you are. You may not be able to see what devious plans they have for your life, but God doesn't want you to fall victim to their schemes.

Repentance and forgiveness are the greatest ways to get delivered from demonic influences because they cleanse your life of those dark forces. However, there are other steps as well.

SIN AND INIQUITY

The Bible talks about sin and iniquity and most people think they're the same, but they're not. Sins are those things that you do wrong; iniquities are the sins of your forefathers that are often passed down from one generation to another.

"Wait a minute, Mike," you might say, "do you mean I'm responsible for what my great, great, great grandfather did? I don't even know his name! I don't know where he lived! I don't know how he died! I don't even know where he was buried!"

You're not responsible for his sins directly, but that iniquity tainted the spiritual DNA that was passed down from generation to generation all the way down to you and to your children. You see the results of this all the time in both positive and negative ways. For instance, let's say your great, great, great grandfather was an alcoholic. That spiritual genetic tendency toward alcoholism is the result of iniquity being passed down from one generation to another. If you traced back your genealogy, you would find it dotted with alcoholism.

The same principle works in blessings. You've seen families, and may be a part of one, where the generations from great, great grandfather all the way down to the great grandchildren are marked by successful doctors, lawyers, pharmacists, businessmen, or ministers.

While you benefit from the blessings passed down to you, the iniquity passed down your generational line can weaken your armor and make you susceptible to the wiles of the enemy. You can deal with generational iniquity by repenting of any known or unknown sins in your family line and praying in the mighty name of Jesus for the blood of Christ, which washes away sin, to be applied to your bloodlines, breaking the chain of sin and iniquity. It is your right as a son or daughter of God to cleanse your bloodlines and allow the supernatural blessings of God to flow.

In Psalm 66:18–19, the Bible tells us that if there is a sin we refuse to turn from, God has the option of not hearing our prayers. "If I had cherished sin in my heart, the Lord would not have listened; but God has surely listened and heard my voice in prayer."

That's why I believe in being quick to repent, quick to forgive, and quick to deal with any generational iniquity that the Lord reveals to me. If you do the same, it will keep the supernatural power of God flowing in your life, which means you can win every battle.

CLEANSING THE LAND

The next layer of cleansing involves the land. Our land and homes are important because that's where we live, grow our crops, and raise our families. There is also a connection between God and the land. The Bible says that after Cain killed his brother, Abel, that Abel's blood cried out to the Lord from the land. Sin and iniquity in the land will open the door to the powers of darkness until someone deals with it.

Psychologists have studied houses where the couple who lived there got a divorce, or where there had been child abuse or suicides. Even after those people moved away, the same problems were repeated over and over in the house. Why did that happen? It happened because no one ever dealt with the sin or iniquity on the land and in the house.

For instance, I live on 10 acres with a house and a barn. When I bought the property, I had no idea what may have happened there over the years, perhaps even before Oklahoma became a state. There could have been a murder or a lynching when some early settler took justice in his own hands. So I took a bottle of anointing oil and said, "Lord, today we're going to cleanse the land." I felt a sense of jubilation as though God were pleased.

I walked the perimeter of the entire property and anointed every fence post while praying that God would forgive any sin or iniquity on the land. I prayed that Jesus' blood would cleanse it. I used my authority in Christ to proclaim that all darkness and demonic spirits had to leave. Remember I am not a preacher, I am a businessman.

> The principles in this chapter work the exact same way for you personally as they do for your home, your property, and your business.

Then I anointed my house, praying to forgive any sin or iniquity. I anointed every door and window using my authority in Christ to cleanse it from all darkness and demonic spirits. A new peace settled over the house and property as I invited the presence of the Holy Spirit to rest there. I know that just as God loves me, He also loves my home and property. He inhabits it because the darkness is gone, and He has been invited to dwell there. I know that His angels are encamped there to guard and protect us.

CLEANSING YOUR BUSINESS

The principles in this chapter work the exact same way for you personally as they do for your home, your property, and your business. It isn't just people and land that needs to be cleansed; large corporations, limited liability companies, or the little coffee shop on the corner all need to be cleansed of darkness. This is real.

Right now General Motors has received billions of dollars from Congress but still filed for bankruptcy. Chrysler is already bankrupt, and Ford is under great pressure to stay alive. They're giant companies whose bottom line affects millions of peoples' jobs, health insurance, and pension plans. Let's use them as an example of how this same principle works in business.

After World War II, Studebaker was the first company to release a new post-war car. However, Preston Tucker was nipping at their heels with a new car the likes of which nobody had ever seen. His car, the 1948 Tucker Sedan, also called the Tucker Torpedo, had an air-cooled, flat six rear engine, disc brakes, fuel injection, a windshield made of shatterproof glass, all instruments on the steering wheel, and a padded dashboard. In addition to being safe, the car was beautiful, stylish, and affordable.

While still struggling with production costs, in June 1949, Preston Tucker and seven of his associates were hauled into court on charges of mail fraud, stock irregularities, and conspiracy to defraud. Until his death, Tucker claimed that the Big Three—Chrysler, General Motors, and Ford—and their supporters were behind the trumped up charges, because he was a threat to their control of the market.

The trial drug on until January 1950 when the jury found Tucker and his associates innocent of all charges. However, the cost of his legal defense and all those strategic months away from his new company left Tucker bankrupt. His reputation had been destroyed, and he was forced to sell his 51 vehicles before shutting his plant.

Tucker's story was made into the movie *The Man and His Dream*, starring Jeff Bridges, produced by George Lucas and directed by Francis Ford Coppola. There was a reference to the Tucker Torpedo in the song, "The Big Three Killed My Baby."

60 YEARS OF INIQUITY

Let's suppose for the moment that there was some evidence that pointed to the Big Three for sabotaging Preston Tucker (there is no definitive proof). If Tucker's allegations were true, the men who perpetrated the crime are no longer at the helm of those three auto

WIN EVERY BATTLE

makers. Based on the principles in this book, what if it were true that some 60 years ago Chrysler, General Motors, and Ford lied and cheated to drive out their competition? Knowing that, how much money would have to be poured into those companies to make them viable again?

Here's the answer: If that actually happened, there isn't enough money in the Federal Reserve and Fort Knox combined to make those companies long-term viable. Why? Because if no one has ever repented for what was allegedly done to Preston Tucker, the iniquity that's been passed down for 60 years in those companies has weakened them.

> "If my people, who are called by my name, will humble themselves and pray and seek my face and turn from their wicked ways, then will I hear from heaven and will forgive their sin and will heal their land."
>
> 2 CHRONICLES 7:14

"So, Mike, are you saying there is no hope for those companies if Preston Tucker's allegations were true?"

No. I'm saying that there is no *natural* help for them, including the infusion of billions of dollars. That money might prop them up for a time, as the initial government emergency loan to GM did but soon was exhausted and eventually bankruptcy was declared. However, if Preston Tucker's allegations were true, the real chokehold on their finances is in the invisible, supernatural realm. In that case, the only way to save those companies is by divine intervention.

However, rather than a supernatural rescue of GM, we have seen them sell the Hummer brand to the Chinese for a song. But the Chinese were not interested in saving the Hummer. They bought the brand for the dealerships that came with the purchase—the real estate on prime locations. And they bought it to capture some of the best technology in the world as well as some of the personnel that went with it. You can bet they have plans in mind that could permanently change the automobile industry.

54

So is there any way to get God to perform a miracle and save any of those companies? Absolutely. I know this because God cannot lie, and there is a promise in the Bible that declares, "If my people, who are called by my name, will humble themselves and pray and seek my face and turn from their wicked ways, then will I hear from heaven and will forgive their sin and will heal their land" (2 Chronicles 7:14).

"But, Mike, it says that God will heal their land. It doesn't say anything about healing a business."

HUMBLE YOURSELF BEFORE GOD

This principle and God's promise work the exact same way for your life, your land, or your business. Assuming that Preston Tucker's allegations were true, what might happen if the officials at General Motors were to be so desperate for a miracle that they accepted my corporate challenge? I would fly to Detroit and meet with a hundred of their top executives. If they were serious about saving that business, I would lead them through the same principles in this book. We would start with Surrender. Instead of working retreats, conference tables, and flow charts, each person would have to get his or her own life aligned with God. That means that we would all eat a little carpet as we humbled ourselves before God. Next, everyone would forgive everyone else. The third step would be to get a research team investigating to see if the company ever did wrong—lies, cheating, espionage, bribery, and sabotage; anything wrong or unethical.

When the list, which could be long, was completed, we would humble ourselves before the Lord and repent of every single thing on the list. We'd say, "God, this is what we've done wrong in this company. We and our forefathers have sinned against You. Those iniquities are strangling us, and this company is about to die. These are the things we know we've done wrong, but if there are others, we ask that You reveal them to us so that we can repent. We're humbling ourselves before

You and turning from our wicked ways forever. We humbly ask that You forgive us and heal our company. Save these jobs and rescue all those who've lost their pensions. We will give You all the glory, not taking any of it for ourselves. We're not just doing this for ourselves, but that the whole world will know that there is a God in heaven, and that You are still doing miracles today."

That's like adding nitroglycerin to your prayers.

GOD'S ANSWER

I think God would say, "That's just what I've been waiting for—a remnant of this company who would humble themselves and repent. I hereby forgive these sins and iniquities, and I will heal your land."

The next step would be to anoint all of General Motor's properties anywhere they existed in the world. Anoint the manufacturing plants, the offices, buildings, and vehicles in order to cleanse the land.

God might wait long enough to intervene to see if they were serious or just looking for a quick fix. If those people kept themselves clean and stayed faithful to the Lord, then...*Bam!* He would drop the answer for a perpetual automobile into the mind of someone in the company. The next day that person would run into the room saying, "I've got it! The idea just dropped in my mind for a battery that will run a car for two years without a charge. You can drive it millions of miles and then plug it into a wall outlet and recharge it."

General Motors would have the patent, and there wouldn't be another car manufacturer in the world still in business. I know this could happen because God controls all technology. The Bible says of Jesus that, "Through him [Jesus] all things were made; without him nothing was made that has been made" (John 1:3).

Without Jesus, nothing is made. That means...*nothing.* There was no spaceship, no automobile, no electricity, no cyberspace made except through Jesus. God has all the answers to every problem the world faces today. He's just waiting on people who will humble themselves, repent, forgive, and cleanse their land.

There is no company so sick that God cannot heal it.

There is no government or nation so evil that God will not forgive and save it.

If we do our part, God will do His part.

When we humble ourselves, repent and turn from our wicked ways, we will win every battle.

BATTLE PLAN

Like little Eddie, we've all been chasing the taxi, carrying our pain and rejection. Like him, in order to be whole, we must face our painful past and forgive. Forgiveness is a key to unlocking the destiny of your individual life and the life of your business. It's the hinge on which all of Christianity turns. If God is going to forgive us for everything we do wrong, He expects no less from us. As hard as this principle can be to accomplish, it brings a rush of divine love, peace, and freedom that will set you on your course to win every battle.

BATTLE PRINCIPLES:

- All of our faith hinges on forgiveness.

- If we don't forgive others, God won't forgive us.

- Forgiveness is mandatory to win every battle.

- Forgiveness has two components. First, we forgive others, and then we must forgive ourselves.

- Forgiveness means surrendering your right to hold anger, bitterness, unforgiveness, judgments, or offenses. It means surrendering the situation to the Living God.

- Once we've repented and forgiven, God looks at us and sees the blood of Jesus and everything we got right.

- Unforgiveness opens spiritual pathways for dark, demonic spirits to wreck havoc in your life.

- True freedom involves dealing with generational iniquity and cleansing the land.
- The principles work the same way for your life, your land, and your business.

BATTLE STRATEGIES:

THE FIRST STEP: *Forgive Others*

Make a list of every hurt you can remember and the people involved. Put your hand over your heart and picture each situation in your mind. Take the memory into your fist and hold it up to God. Say, "Jesus, I give you this situation. You understand it; You experienced it. Take the pain from me now. I forgive this person and release them from my judgments." Now open your fist and give it to God. Do the same thing with every situation on your list. If there is a deliverance ministry in your church, take advantage of it.

THE SECOND STEP: *Forgive Yourself*

Make a list of everything you hold against yourself. Put your hand over your heart and picture each situation in your mind. Take the memory into your fist and hold it up to God. Say, "Jesus, I give you this situation. You understand it; You experienced it. Take the pain from me now. I forgive myself and release myself from this unforgiveness." Now open your fist and give it to God. Do the same thing with every situation on your list.

THE THIRD STEP: *Deal with Generational Iniquities*

Ask God to help you recognize generational iniquities in your family lines. You might ask older family members as well. You can deal with generational iniquity by repenting of any known or unknown sins in your family line and praying in the mighty name of Jesus for the blood of Christ, which washes away sin, to be applied to your bloodlines, breaking the chain of sin and iniquity. It is your right as a son or daughter of God to cleanse your bloodlines and allow the supernatural blessings of God to flow.

THE FOURTH STEP: *Cleanse Your Land*

Take a bottle of oil and anoint all the doors, windows, and anything in your house that the Living God highlights to you. Repent of sin and iniquity and release forgiveness. Use your authority to command all demonic spirits to leave your property. Do the same thing by walking the perimeter of your land. After cleansing the land, ask the Holy Spirit to dwell there.

Repeat each step of the battle plan for your business.

4

WINNING THE WAR OVER FEAR

C licking onto my online banking, I entered my password and waited while the computer pulled up my account information. A moment later, prickles of fear raced up the back of my neck, and it felt as though my hair were standing on end like a cat cornered by a Pit Bull. The analogy was apt. I'd done a huge commercial business deal with a Pit Bull of a man; in comparison, I was a kitten. He was a large man who towered over me by what seemed to be miles. If wealth and power were measured by size, he would be the Empire State Building, and I would be Starbucks. I discovered the hard way that he was a Pit Bull in business, willing to tear anyone to shreds who got too close to his pile of money.

Looking at my account information, it was what *wasn't* there that caused fear to dance an Irish jig on my mind and emotions. My share of our commercial business deal had been $515,000, which isn't chump change to Donald Trump. I wasn't in the Donald Trump category, and that half million dollars meant life or death to my business.

The Pit Bull, whom I will call George from Alabama, still hadn't paid me. The money was long overdue. Taking a deep breath, I picked up the phone and called him.

"Hey, George," I said when he answered, "just checking in to see how things are going with you. I'm glad everything worked out so well on our business deal, and I was wondering when I'm going to get paid."

"I'm not going to pay you."

"Is there a cash flow problem we can work around?"

"No, there's no cash flow problem. I'm just not going to pay you."

"Is there some confusion about the documents we signed? Maybe you have questions about our rights and obligations and who gets what?"

> "No, Mike, there's no confusion. I have the money. I've read the documents. I understand what I owe you. I'm just not going to pay you."

"No, Mike, there's no confusion. I have the money. I've read the documents. I understand what I owe you. I'm just not going to pay you."

"Oh." What do you say to that? I knew better than to try and get tough; he could rip my head off and serve it up on a platter. I made small talk for a couple of minutes and then got off the phone.

THE TASTE OF FEAR

I could taste the fear that tried to overwhelm me. The metallic taste left my mouth dry and turned my mind to silly putty. I realized that I was fighting not one, but two of the deadliest battles of my life. First, without that half million dollars, my new business was toast. It would gasp its last breath, and I'd have to sell my home and leave Oklahoma and our elderly parents in order to take a corporate job somewhere just to survive and keep a roof over our heads.

Justice was on my side; my contract with George was airtight. I'd earned the money, and he didn't have a legal leg to stand on to keep it from me. I'm also an attorney, and I knew that suing a Pit Bull was futile. He had enough money to keep me tied up in court for years while what money I had left would be flushed down the drain in legal fees. Mine was a similar situation to that of Preston Tucker. My opponent had unlimited resources, and having my time and money tied up in court would do nothing except kill my business faster and, like Tucker, possibly bring me to bankruptcy.

> I knew that if I didn't win the war over fear, George was the least of my problems.

He had me cornered, and after looking at the situation from every possible angle, I knew that I had no way out. I was no match for him physically or financially. I didn't know him when we agreed on a joint venture; I had no way of knowing he was ruthless.

That was my first battle; one I saw no way of winning.

My second battle was even more deadly. If George were a Pit Bull, the fear that stalked me was a serial killer who had me in his crosshairs. I knew that if I didn't win the war over fear, George was the least of my problems.

FROZEN IN FEAR LIKE LOCTITE

When I was a kid, I used to build model airplanes using a tiny tube of glue called Loctite. The glue dried in an instant, and once the seal was made, it wouldn't break. If you put the glue on one finger and pressed it into another finger, they'd have to be surgically separated. I understood that Satan uses fear like Loctite. He spills it over your mind and emotions just like Loctite, and it freezes your ability to function. You can't think. You can't move. In business, you have to be creative, coming up with new ideas, new plans, and new clients. You can't do that with fear on you. You won't close a deal, because fear will have you locked so tight you're afraid to move forward. You will be too locked down to think of creative new ideas and patents. Fear will put all your ingenuity in lockdown.

I also understood that while fear affects your emotions, it isn't just an emotion. In numerous places the Bible describes fear as a spirit. One of them is found in 2 Timothy 1:7: "For God has not given us a spirit of fear, but of power and of love and of a sound mind" (NKJV).

The single most repeated admonition in the Bible is God's order that we, "Fear not!" The Bible tells us 365 times not to be afraid; once for every day of the year. Why do you suppose the Bible screams that message? It's because the spirit of fear is like a terrorist who will capture you and torture you before he kills you.

The Bible also makes it clear that fear brings torment. "There is no fear in love; but perfect love casts out fear, because *fear involves torment*" (1 John 4:18 NKJV, emphasis mine).

To understand just how demonic fear is, that spirit entered the Garden of Eden the moment Adam sinned. After he sinned, Adam said, "I was afraid." Adam and Eve had never known fear until that moment.

GOING ON THE OFFENSE

That's the reason I knew that as bad as the situation was with George, losing a half million dollars wasn't Satan's ultimate goal. He wanted me to cave in to a spirit of fear, which would freeze my mind and emotions as though he'd dumped a gallon of Loctite over my head. Then he would torment me while he kept my finances in a stranglehold. But it wasn't just my business he wanted to destroy. He wanted to take my life and destroy my family.

I was on the devil's Most Wanted List. Don't feel sorry for me— so are you. We're in a war against an unseen enemy whose greatest ploy is to keep us so blinded that we're oblivious to what he's doing.

I was on the defensive, and I knew I had to turn the tables and go after that spirit of fear. There are no natural weapons with the power to take out a spiritual foe; no gun, no knife, no rocket launcher or atomic bomb. But there are spiritual weapons that will blast them out of our territory. Those weapons may seem foolish to some people, but it's only because they don't understand their enemy's weakness.

I knew his weakness. Before he rebelled against God and was cast out of heaven, the Bible says that Lucifer was beautiful, covered with precious stones and musical instruments were formed in him. Before he became puffed up with pride, he had been created to make music and praise God in heaven. Ezekiel 28:12–16 (NKJV) gives us a glimpse into our enemy, who was once an anointed cherub:

"Thus says the Lord GOD: 'You were the seal of perfection, full of wisdom and perfect in beauty. You were in Eden, the garden of God; every precious stone was your covering:the sardius, topaz, and diamond, beryl, onyx, and jasper, sapphire, turquoise, and emerald with gold. The workmanship of your timbrels and pipes was pre-pared for you on the day you were created. You were the anointed cherub who covers; I established you; you were on the holy moun-tain of God; you walked back and forth in the midst of fiery stones. You were perfect in your ways from the day you were created, till in-iquity was found in you. By the abundance of your trading you be-came filled with violence within, and you sinned; therefore I cast you as a profane thing out of the mountain of God; and I destroyed you, O covering cherub, from the midst of the fiery stones.'"

Isaiah 14:12–15 (NKJV) also described Lucifer's fall from heaven: "How you are fallen from heaven, O Lucifer, son of the morning! How you are cut down to the ground, you who weakened the na-tions! For you have said in your heart: 'I will ascend into heaven, I will exalt my throne above the stars of God; I will also sit on the mount of the congregation. On the farthest sides of the north; I will ascend above the heights of the clouds, I will be like the Most High.' Yet you shall be brought down to Sheol, to the lowest depths of the Pit."

THE WEAPONS OF OUR WARFARE

One important strategy to winning any battle is to know your enemy's weakness and attack his Achilles' heel. Before he rebelled against God, Lucifer had been something like the worship leader, making music and praising God on His holy mountain. Now he craves that worship for himself; he can't stand hearing praise and worship to God. This is true for every demonic spirit, including the spirit of fear. Praise and worship to God is like pouring spiritual acid over them, and they have to flee.

Therefore, when I got off the phone with George, and I felt fear pouring Loctite over my mind and emotions, I understood two things: the battle against fear was mine to fight, and I would have to depend on God to deal with George.

I went on the offensive by praising God. "Father," I said, "I worship You! You alone are God; You're the Living God, the God of Abraham, Isaac, and Jacob. You alone are worthy of my praise and adoration. I want to thank You for Your love and faithfulness to me since the moment You formed me in my mother's womb. Thank You that You rejoice over me with singing. Thank You for leading me and directing my steps. Thank You for my wife and son. Thank You for our extended family. Thank You for those in spiritual leadership over me. Thank You, Jesus, for giving Your life on the cross to pay the price for my sins. Thank You for defeating death, hell, and the grave. Thank You for raising Christ from the dead and seating Him at Your own right hand. Thank You that I am in Christ Jesus, an heir to Your Kingdom."

I put on praise music and sang praises to God. I could feel the Loctite dissolving from my mind and emotions, and I could almost hear the spirit of fear screaming in agony as it ran like a scalded dog. The Bible says that God inhabits the praises of His people, which meant that when I praised God, He showed up along with His angelic host. Knowing that I had a great cloud of witnesses, I did the same thing that Jesus did when the devil tempted Him in the wilderness. Instead of spewing doubt and unbelief, I spoke the Word of God over my situation.

SPIRITUAL LAWS

"Father, You never promised that weapons wouldn't be formed against me, but You did promise that no weapon formed against me would prosper. You said, 'No weapon formed against you shall prosper, and every tongue which rises against you in judgment you shall condemn. This is the heritage of the servants of the LORD, and their righteousness is from Me,' says the LORD" (Isaiah 54:17 NKJV).

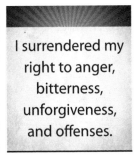
I surrendered my right to anger, bitterness, unforgiveness, and offenses.

"Father," I prayed, "George owes me $515,000, and he has refused to pay me. I've looked at this from every angle, and I see no human way to force him into doing what is right. I'm surrendered to You; every atom of my being and all that I have are Yours. So I'm giving this problem to You. I ask that You win this battle for me."

I didn't hear an audible voice telling me what to do. I didn't hear the Lord say anything. I just believed that because I'd asked, God would answer. My job was to fight off fear, so I continued to praise and worship God, spending time meditating on His promises in the Bible and speaking them over my situation.

I also knew that no matter how much my emotions screamed for the right to be angry, I couldn't afford it. I surrendered my right to anger, bitterness, unforgiveness, and offenses. "Lord, I just want You to know that I have forgiven George. I release him and this entire situation to You."

MAKING CONTACT

A week later, I phoned George again. Keeping my attitude upbeat and pleasant, I said, "Hi, George, how are you doing? It's good to talk to you again. Listen, I was just checking to see how you were coming with my payment."

"I think we've already been through this, Mike," he said. "I'm not going to pay you."

"Okay, well, you have a great day, George."

I waited a week and phoned him again. Staying upbeat and pleasant, I asked how my payment was coming.

> Fear tried to tap dance on my head, but I shook it off like a dog after a run through the sprinkler.

"Mike, I don't know what part of this you don't understand. Let me make myself perfectly clear. I know I owe you $515,000, but I'm not going to pay it. I'm *never* going to pay you that money!"

I called him the next week...and the next, but he never budged in his decision. I called him every week for 10 weeks. The tenth time I called, he went nuclear.

"Hey, George," I said, "I'm just checking in to see how my payment is coming."

He screamed at me, and I didn't need a video phone to know that his face was scarlet and he looked like he was going to explode and kill anyone within range. "I'm tired of you calling me!" he screamed. "I'm *not going to pay you! In fact, let me tell you how much I'm not going to pay you! I'm coming to Oklahoma to tell you to your face!*"

Fear tried to tap dance on my head, but I shook it off like a dog after a run through the sprinkler. "Okay," I said, "let's set a date."

We set a date for a week later, and then he picked up where he'd left off. "I'm coming, and we're going to end this once and for all! I'm going to tell you to your face that I'll *never* pay you what I owe you, and then I don't ever want to hear from you again!"

"Great," I said. "I'll see you in a week."

FACING THE GIANT

I called the airport and reserved a little room for our meeting.

On the appointed day, I drove to the airport and said, "God, you know I'm not big enough to deal with this. He'd squash me like a bug. This is the battle between the Titan and the tiny, and he's the Titan. However, You are on my side, and that's all that matters. You're big enough to deal with him. You promised that if I would surrender every cell of myself to You that You would protect and defend me. I don't know how You're going to do it, but I need Your divine intervention to win this battle."

I knew George wasn't coming to greet me with his checkbook and a warm hug. He was coming to humiliate me and intimidate me so that I would never dare disturb him again. I'll admit that I trembled walking into the airport. I fought fear by putting one foot in front of the other. I kept going. I didn't let the fear freeze me with Loctite. I reminded myself that God was bigger than George. I believed with every fiber of my being that God was with me, and that He would rescue me.

I stood in the airport and watched him walking toward me. This had to be what David felt like when he squared off with the giant Goliath. Without God, he must have known he was toast.

"Hi, George," I said. He mumbled something and followed me to the little room I'd rented. I could feel his fury as he stormed into the room and sat on one side of the table. I took the seat opposite him and wondered what in the world I should say. Since I had no idea what to say, I didn't say anything.

BE STILL AND KNOW THAT I AM GOD

No more than six seconds had passed since we sat down, but I was stunned to see that his face was no longer beet red. He was staring at something just above my head, and all the color had drained out of his face. It was as white as 10,000 sheets of Xerox paper—white,

white, white. It was so white that I was alarmed. *He's either had a stroke or a heart attack, and he's going to die right here!* I thought, fighting panic. I did *not* want this man to die on my watch; here in the conference room alone with me. *Maybe I should call an ambulance.*

I opened my mouth to ask if he was okay, but the power of God checked me. It was as though the Lord put His hand over my mouth and whispered in my ear, *"Don't talk. Be quiet. Let me handle this."*

> I opened my mouth to ask if he was okay, but the power of God checked me.

I swallowed the words and said nothing. I watched him while he continued to stare at something above my head. No one spoke, and I felt awkward and uncomfortable. Time passed so slow that it seemed to stand still. I never remember feeling so out of my element. *What if he died? What if he was so angry he'd had a stroke? What was going on?* My mind raced trying to make sense of the situation, but I didn't speak. Neither did George.

I couldn't take my eyes off of him. After a while, I saw his shoulders slump. A few minutes later, he started to mumble. I strained to understand what he said. It sounded something like, "Uhh-hhh...wwweee'll ppay yyouuu." *Did he say what I think he said?* I wanted to ask him to try again, but I knew I wasn't to speak.

Another five minutes crawled by, each agonizing second seeming like an eternity in the silence. I saw his shoulders move up a bit. Color began creeping back into his face. A few minutes later, he looked almost normal. He pulled his gaze away from whatever he'd been looking at above my head and looked at me.

"Well, I think I'll go back to Alabama," he said.

"Okay, George." Those were the only two words I'd spoken the entire time. George stood up and walked out the door and down the hall. I've never seen him since that day.

Two days later, I clicked onto my online banking and entered my password. A moment later, a chill rippled up my back between my shoulder blades before racing up my neck to my scalp. There had been a wire transfer into my account in the amount of $515,000.

GOD INTERSECTS WITH MAN

I am as in awe of God today as I write this story as I was the day it happened. I am here to tell you that there is a Living God who is still very much in the miracle business. What did He do to convince George to pay me? The truth is that I don't know, and I may never know this side of heaven. My best guess is that He opened George's eyes into the spirit realm and let him see either the angel that stood guard over me or a glimpse of the Lord Himself. Whatever he saw scared him so much that it was worth a half million dollars to get as far away from it as possible.

> There had been a wire transfer into my account in the amount of $515,000.

I have a good friend who tried to reason with me not long ago. He said, "Mike, come on! It's not *possible* to win every battle. Get real!"

I have to tell you that it's far too late for me to believe that. I've experienced too many situations similar to the one I just described. But I will get real about it. Here's the truth: It's not humanly possible to win every battle. It wasn't humanly possible for me to win that battle with George. However, I'm not saying that we can win every battle in our own human strength. What I'm saying is that each of us can have a relationship with the Living God who brings His power into our everyday lives. With God's supernatural intervention, it's impossible to lose.

We all know that there are laws that govern life here on earth. One of them is the law of gravity. Unless you override the law of gravity with the law of thrust and lift that operates an aircraft, you will fall every single time you get airborne.

The problem that most of us have had with the supernatural is that we didn't know what laws governed that area or how to operate within their boundaries. We've read about miracles, and in some cases we've seen miracles, but the chance of getting a miracle seemed less than the chance of winning the lottery. The whole miracle thing seemed like a crap shoot, which is why people got under the impression that you could ask for a miracle, but unless God was in a really good mood, it would never happen.

That's not the case! The spiritual laws that govern the supernatural are as concrete as the law of gravity. We just haven't known what they were and how to operate in them. Perhaps a more honest answer would be that some of us have glimpsed them in the Bible, but deep down inside we thought they were stupid. *There are invisible forces at work to try and destroy me? Sounds like the Twilight Zone. Total, unconditional surrender to God? Don't be absurd. What do you mean I have to forgive? Are you kidding me? Who would expect such a thing? I will never forgive that jerk, and I'm sure God understands. Come on, He'd be just as mad. And that whole thing about fear being some spiritual woo-woo. Get real—fear is just an emotion that God gave us to keep us out of trouble. Some people take the Bible so literally. You just have to take what's relevant for this century. I hate it that I've got to try to find a job and start over. I don't know why my last two businesses failed. At least I've learned from my mistakes. Oh well, the third time's a charm!* There are a lot of people who say things just like that, and there are others who just think that way. God is ready and waiting with supernatural intervention in their lives, but they're trying to get a miracle while defying spiritual laws, and it isn't going to happen.

> The spiritual laws that govern the supernatural are as concrete as the law of gravity.

MANIFESTATIONS OF FEAR

The purpose of this chapter was to present one of the most important spiritual principles necessary to win every battle. You have to win the war over fear. Fear is a very powerful spirit that manifests in many ways. Believe it or not, studies have shown that the number one fear people face is the fear of public speaking. The one that comes in at second place is the fear of dying. That means that there are a lot of people who'd rather die than speak before a crowd. I don't know how other fears are rated, but high on the list would be the fear of failure and the fear of rejection. People are afraid of economic downturns. They're afraid of losing their job, their health insurance, or their retirement. Some people are even frozen with Loctite due to the fear of success. Many people are afraid of social situations. Others are afraid of spiders, snakes, or even Lady Bugs. Fear can manifest as a sense of dread, anxiety, or nervousness. The symptoms can be anywhere from mild to debilitating.

However fear manifests in your life, you must realize that behind it is a demonic spirit as dangerous as an assassin. "Wait a minute," someone said, "what are you some kind of maniac preacher?"

No, I'm a businessman, a really good businessman. I'm a resurrected, Spirit-filled, successful businessman who refuses to fear. I am a man who has tapped into the supernatural power of God to win every battle, and I would like nothing more than to see you do the same thing. In order to do that, you've got to fight fear. When George tried to steal a half million dollars from me, that was a real pucker factor. I was surrendered to God. I had forgiven everyone I knew to forgive, including myself. God was backstage ready to deal with the situation. But if I hadn't won the war over fear, my miracle would have been stopped in its tracks.

STEPS TO WINNING THE WAR AGAINST FEAR

The first and most important weapon when dealing with fear is to praise God. Put on praise music. Sing to Him. Thank God for everything He's done in your life. If fear is still tap dancing on your head, start over and do it again.

The second weapon in your arsenal when battling fear is the Word of God. According to the Bible, God's Word is alive, sharper than a two-edged sword. Speaking God's promises over yourself and your situation will trigger faith; and faith is the antidote for fear.

Another weapon in your arsenal is to use your authority in Christ Jesus. Speak to that spirit of fear and say, "Father, I repent of cooperating with the spirit of fear. I renounce all fear in my life. I bind, muzzle, and gag the spirit of fear. In the name of Jesus, spirit of fear I command you to go!" As children by the age of five, we all developed a fear of man. In order to move into the supernatural, we must renounce the fear of man.

> The first and most important weapon when dealing with fear is to praise God.

If fear is a stronghold in your life or family, find a good deliverance ministry that comes well recommended and get the help you need to get rid of it. Stay submitted to your local church where you have prayer cover and listen to sermons and teaching tapes that will build your faith.

I grew up in a home where my parents planted seeds of fear in my life. Their ongoing message was, "You just never know when something bad is going to happen." In the mind of a child that translated into a message of perpetual doom. "You never know what's going to happen. You could be in a car wreck, so don't wear ratty underwear."

Bill Hybels, minister of Willow Creek Community Church in Chicagoland, discipled me from afar. He once preached a message called, "You Just Never Know." Only his message was one of hope: He said that God is so good you just never know when He's going to do something wonderful just to bless you. That truth changed my life, and I hope it will change yours.

That is the truth. Never forget that God's love is trillions of times more powerful than any fear. God's love is to fear what light is to darkness. The light displaces the darkness in the same manner that

God's love displaces fear. When you get a revelation of that love, fear cannot remain, for love and fear cannot coexist. Fear has to go. When you learn to give fear no place in your life, you're on your way to winning every battle.

BATTLE PLAN

There's nothing like having $515,000 stolen and your business about to take a nose dive from which it will never recover to make the strongest man quake with fear like a little girl. I was fighting one of the costliest battles of my life, but everything hinged on my ability to win the war over fear. It doesn't matter what kind of battle you're facing; it may be a battle against disease, a battle against an addiction, a battle over your finances, or a battle to save your children. In every battle, you've got to win the war against fear.

BATTLE PRINCIPLES:

- The spirit of fear is the enemy's first line of defense.
- Fear will freeze your ability to make good decisions just as if a gallon of Loctite had been poured over your mind and emotions.
- In the Bible, God tells us 365 times not to be afraid. That's once for every day of the year.
- Fear brings torment.
- Only spiritual weapons will win the war against the spirit of fear.
- The spiritual laws that govern the supernatural world are as concrete as the law of gravity.

BATTLE STRATEGIES:

THE FIRST STEP: Praise and Worship

The moment fear starts tap dancing on your head, begin to praise and worship God. The spirit of fear will run like a scalded dog.

THE SECOND STEP: *The Word of God*
The Word of God is alive and sharper than a two-edged sword. Read and meditate on God's Word because it will build your faith, and faith is the antidote for fear.

THE THIRD STEP: *Speak God's Words*
When Jesus was tempted by the devil in the wilderness, He defeated the enemy by speaking only God's words. You can defeat any spiritual force by speaking God's words over the situation.

THE FOURTH STEP: *Use Your Spiritual Authority*
When Jesus ascended into heaven, He delegated His authority to believers. Speak to that spirit of fear and say, "Father, I repent of cooperating with the spirit of fear. I renounce all fear in my life. I bind, muzzle, and gag the spirit of fear. In the name of Jesus, spirit of fear, I command you to go!"

THE FIFTH STEP: *Act with Courage in the Face of Fear*
When I walked into the airport that day, I didn't feel brave. But real courage is moving ahead with what you know to do in the face of fear.

THE SIXTH STEP: *Let the Holy Spirit Lead You*
Spend time getting to know the nudges of the Holy Spirit, and then do whatever He says. In the situation with George, God required me to be quiet and not speak. Sometimes you just have to get out of God's way. Let Him lead you.

OBEDIENCE
BRINGS BLESSINGS

Making a dash for my car, the air was so frigid that my molars shivered in their sockets. Getting used to northern winters was only one of the stressors in my life. In order to avoid stress, authorities say that you shouldn't group a lot of major life changes together in a single year. My stress chart must have spiked like the national debt. I'd taken a corporate job with Kohl's Department Stores, Inc., which meant I was trying to navigate my way through a new company, learning a whole new management team and their philosophy. That would have been stressful enough, but my new position required that we move to Milwaukee. When we lived in California, and to a lesser degree Oklahoma, people were outside a lot. Neighbors wandered from lawn to lawn, drinking iced tea, grocery stores stayed busy, and it was easy to meet people almost anywhere we went. Although there were some brave souls who spent their free time driving snowmobiles and cross-country skiing, winter in Milwaukee meant that most people stayed indoors. There weren't lines of people waiting to check out at the grocery store because people tended to stock up on supplies.

The result for us newcomers was loneliness.

In addition, we were expecting our first child, which brought with it the added stress of finding a safe place to live. At that time, the residential real estate market was nonexistent. There was *nothing* for sale, and we weren't even looking for new construction; we hoped to find an older home. So many people wanted to buy homes that they were usually sold by word of mouth before a For Sale sign ever made it into the front yard. Meanwhile, we were living in an apartment that was not located in a safe part of town.

> "I'd like an older, Mediterranean style house with tile roof and a view of Milwaukee. There *isn't* a house like that here, but You asked what I wanted, and *that's* what I want!"

The further along we got in the pregnancy, the more desperate I felt about getting settled in a safe place before the baby arrived. With the pressure of my new job, the absence of family and friends nearby, and the fact that we could find no safe place to live, I felt frustrated beyond belief. I hated driving to work and leaving my wife alone in that neighborhood. Yet I felt powerless to do anything about it.

TEMPORARY SURRENDER

The temperature plunged so low that it felt as though hell had finally frozen over. I pulled to a stop at a traffic light and realized that I had reached the end of myself. Gritting my teeth, and with less than an ideal attitude, I cried out to God.

"God, we need a house, and we need it *now!*"

Alone in the car, I was jolted when I heard an audible voice.

"Mike, what kind of house do you want?"

Who said that? I realized it was the Voice of the Living God. *The Voice!*

I was upset…and perhaps a tiny bit arrogant…when in exasperation I said, "I'd like an older, Mediterranean style house with a tile roof and a view of Milwaukee." I stomped my foot on the floorboard for emphasis and continued. "There *isn't* a house like that here, but You asked what I wanted, and *that's* what I want!"

Total silence. The Living God had spoken to me in an audible voice, and while I'd been honest, I'd acted like a jerk. Now it appeared that God had nothing else to say to me. I drove to work in silence.

In telling the story, I could have cleaned up that incident and made myself sound better and more spiritual than I was. I chose to tell the unvarnished truth because I want you to believe me when I tell you that I was far from perfect then, and I'm far from perfect now. That moment was one of a long line of temporary surrenders. Whenever I found myself in a situation that I was powerless to fix, I cried out to God for intervention. Once God intervened, I then took back the reins of my life, unaware that by total surrender I could go from living crisis to crisis to enjoying God's intervention in even the most mundane things in my everyday life.

Certain that I'd not only offended God, but asked for something that didn't exist, I plotted my strategy to find a house. I asked Kohl's for permission to attach my business card to a letter asking people to keep us in mind if they knew of anyone selling their home. When Kohl's approved my request, we found a nice, safe area and blitzed them with our letters. Then we hoped for the best.

THE GOD OF DETAILS

Less than a week later, I arrived at my office and found a voicemail waiting for me. "Mike Galiga," a man's voice said, "this is Dr. Kent. I've got your card here, and thought I should call you because we're going to sell our house." In the message, he repeated three different times that he had a very strong feeling that he should call me. He didn't give any details of his house, but left his phone number.

I almost speed dialed his number.

"That was quick!" Dr. Kent said when I reached him. "We're moving our medical practice to Madera, California, out in the central valley." We visited for a while, and he told me how excited he was about the move and how *un*excited his wife was to leave because they had a beautiful home in a great neighborhood with lots of friends.

I listened for about 15 minutes before saying, "Dr. Kent, could you tell me a little bit about your house?"

"Oh, sorry!" he said. "Well, it was built in 1922, and it's called an Italian Renaissance Revival. It has an Italian Mediterranean tile roof and a nice view of downtown Milwaukee."

My knees buckled, and I fell back into my chair.

I made an appointment to see the house, got off the phone, and said, "God, I knew You spoke to me at that intersection the other day. I was frustrated and a little bit arrogant, and I'm sorry."

He forgave me.

I was shocked when we pulled up in front of Dr. Kent's house. It was the home of our dreams. The view of downtown Milwaukee was there alright. Fifteen minutes later, we shook hands on a price. Within three days, it was under contract. Several months later, we moved in.

FAVOR AND OBEDIENCE

I share this story because it is an excellent example of two things: the blessings of God and the favor of God. Let's start with the concept of favor, because people tend to confuse the love of God with the favor of God. In order to understand, let me share an important principle. God loves all of His children equally, but He doesn't favor them equally. Why? Because love is unconditional, but favor is linked to obedience.

For example, imagine that you had 10 children. You love each of them so much that sometimes you ache when you look at them. Ten children create a mountain of challenges and problems, but you can't imagine your life without any of them. There's something special about each of them; you can see their gifts and talents emerging from a young age. You're delighted to watch them grow and mature.

> God loves all of His children equally, but He doesn't favor them equally.

However, as much as you love them all, you don't always favor them the same. For instance, each child is required to clean his or her room on Saturday. They have to pick up their dirty clothes and take them to the laundry hamper. They're supposed to make their beds and put away all their toys, sports equipment, bug collections, and science projects. There's always a lot of grumbling and complaining, but because they're anxious to go have fun, most of them get their chores done as fast as possible. The covers on their beds might not be straight, the clean clothes may not be folded well, and the dirty clothes may have made it to the laundry room floor instead of into the hamper, but they put some effort into it.

MISCHIEVOUS MAX

Then there's Max. You love this kid because he has his mother's eyes and most of her good traits, but he works hard at disobedience. His clothes never make it to the laundry room. When he runs out of anything to wear, you follow the stench and find piles of dirty underwear, socks, his baseball uniform, and the new suit you bought him to wear in a wedding all crumpled up and stuffed under his bed. Instead of putting his baseball gloves, bats, skis, and helmets where they belong, you open his closet door and they fall on you like a mudslide. The only reason his bed gets made is that he threatens and bullies one of the younger kids and makes them do it. You've talked to him; you've counseled with him; you've prayed with him; you've grounded him and made him apologize. Max, however, has set his back teeth in a way that lets you know that he is determined to outlast you, outsmart you, and take his rebellion to a whole new level. For the past two years, Max has made not obeying his career goal. You can't depend on him to do anything that he's asked to do.

When Max and his twin sister, Melissa, are both invited to go on a band trip to London, you sit down and take a hard look at the situation. Max can force such beautiful music out of a saxophone that you want to cry. He's a gifted musician, there's no doubt about it. Playing against the competition in London would be a great steppingstone for him.

> That's the difference between love and favor; love is unconditional, but favor is earned through obedience.

Here's the rub: you love Max and Melissa the same, but you don't favor them the same. For one thing, Melissa not only does what you ask, she notices when her mother is tired and picks up extra chores without being asked. She's quick to obey everyone in authority, and you know that she won't give the band chaperons a minute of trouble.

Then there's Max—you love the kid so much that you'd lay down your life for him, but you know without a doubt that he'll see it as a challenge to break every rule while he's on the trip to London. What do you do? You write out a check for Melissa to go to London; Max will be in summer school making up for all the classes he skipped.

That's the difference between love and favor; love is unconditional, but favor is earned through obedience.

LAW OF THE LIFEGUARD

I learned the difference as a kid when, during seven summers, I made an awesome rise in power at the local country club. I started as the pool boy and worked my way up to head lifeguard. Each swimming pool has a set of rules, all of them centered on safety. For instance, you can't run around the pool on wet cement, because it's only a matter of time until you slip, fall, and crack your head open like a ripe watermelon. You can't bring glass pitchers of lemonade to the pool area, because if you drop it and it breaks, a lot of barefoot kids could get hurt. If you don't follow the rules, the lifeguard will blow the whistle and you have to get out of the pool.

I whistled hundreds and hundreds of kids out of the pool and made them sit out for a while. Why any kid would want to sit in the hot sun while everyone else swam and laughed and had fun was beyond me. Yet that's what happened. A lot of them couldn't seem to break out of the cycle of disobedience even though it meant they spent a good portion of the summer sitting on the sidelines alone. I watched them like a two-headed monkey and wondered why they couldn't just obey a few simple rules and stay in the water with their friends.

> I whistled hundreds and hundreds of kids out of the pool and made them sit out for a while. Why any kid would want to sit in the hot sun while everyone else swam and laughed and had fun was beyond me.

As an adult, I noticed the same patterns in many people's lives. Okay, I'll be honest; I noticed it first in my own life. I realized that my own choices to obey or disobey God's rules caused me to cycle in and out of blessings. I started paying attention to what tripped me up and what helped me out of those cycles, and then I started watching it happen in the lives of other people around me. The people who colored between the lines of God's rules seemed to enjoy more blessings and fewer problems. Others, like the hard-headed kids at the pool, couldn't seem to get off of the treadmill of disobedience even though they suffered the consequences time and time again.

Although I'm sure this isn't original, I recognized patterns that I call cycles of blessings and other patterns that I call cycles of the curse. Our behavior patterns drive each cycle in the direction of a clock.

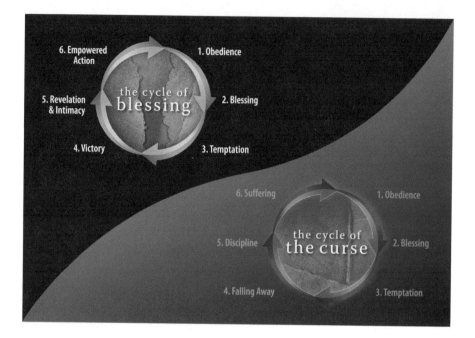

CYCLE OF THE CURSE

For instance, the cycle of the curse begins at 12:00 with obedience. Obedience brought the favor of God, which in turn brought the blessings of God. So at 3:00, the person in the cycle of the curse enjoys the blessings. Then, right on the heels of the blessings, at 6:00, is temptation. Everyone is tempted by something every day, but it's what you do with those temptations that determines whether or not you enjoy the blessings of God. As adults, a lot of us do the same thing those kids did over and over: When temptation arose, they took the bait.

The Bible says that sin is only enjoyable for a season, and for the kids I whistled out of the pool, that season lasted about 60 seconds. In other situations, they might enjoy the forbidden fruit a bit longer. In the cycle of the curse, I describe taking the bait as Falling Away, which means that your choice takes you away from the blessings of God. Falling Away brings the Discipline of God, followed by Suffering.

In the lifeguard analogy, the cycle of the curse looked something like this:

1. *Obedience.* Kid is playing in the pool, splashing friends, and having fun.
2. *Blessing.* Because he is obeying the rules, he enjoys my blessing and gets to continue having fun.
3. *Temptation.* Temptation beacons him to break the rules. *Come on! Just do it! It'll be fun! He probably won't even see you!*
4. *Falling Away.* He takes the bait and runs across the wet cement.
5. *Discipline.* He has lost all favor with me, and before he lands the great cannonball he had planned, the whistle screams and everyone at the pool is frozen in place, waiting to see who will be disciplined.
6. *Suffering.* He suffers alone in the hot sun while the cutest girl in fifth grade plays water volleyball with his best friend.

CYCLE OF BLESSING

The cycle of blessing begins the exact same way with Obedience at 12:00, Blessing at 3:00, and Temptation at 4:00. The difference is that when temptation comes knocking, no one takes the bait. I didn't say it was easy, but, like anything else, it can become a lifestyle. Resisting the temptation brings Victory. At 7:00, on the heels of Victory, is a time of intimacy with God that results in fresh revelation. The new revelation from heaven brings Empowered Action at 11:00.

In the lifeguard analogy, the cycle of blessing would like this:

1. *Obedience.* Kid is playing in the pool, splashing friends, and having fun.
2. *Blessing.* Because he is obeying the rules, he enjoys my blessing and gets to continue having fun.
3. *Temptation.* Temptation beacons him to break the rules. *Come on! Just do it! It'll be fun! He probably won't even see you!*
4. *Victory.* He is *so* tempted that he almost takes the bait, but

before he does, he looks up at me. I'm watching him. I've blown the whistle over him so many times I can see what he's thinking before he acts on it. When he makes eye contact with me, I know he's thinking, and I give him a thumb's up.

5. *Revelation and Intimacy.* He goes back to having fun, but when I get my next break, he sidles over and sits beside me. I tell him about how I started as a pool boy when I wasn't much older than he is, and how I worked my way up to head lifeguard. I tell him that he would make a great lifeguard someday, and I explain that I'm concerned about the little kids who could get knocked into the pool when the bigger kids get too rowdy.

6. *Empowered to Action.* He goes back to having fun but keeps a new, watchful eye on the little kids around him. A couple of hours later, he sees a toddler get knocked into the water by some kids who aren't paying attention to what they're doing. Before I can get the whistle to my mouth, he swoops in and grabs the terrified child out of the pool. The frantic mother can't thank him enough and tells the club management about how he saved her daughter. The boy is given a commendation and a gift. The other kids look up to him. He now has favor with everyone at the club, adults and children alike.

TEMPTATION IS THE STUMBLING BLOCK

In both cycles, the first half is the same: Obedience, Blessing, and Temptation. The choices we make when temptation woos us determine the difference between cycling into Discipline and Suffering or cycling into Victory, Revelation and Intimacy, and Empowered Action.

These cycles, and the favor that comes with obedience, explain why the measure of God's blessing varies from person to person. The good news is that you can break out of the cycle of the curse and live in the cycle of blessing.

"Look, Mike, you don't understand. I've tried everything, and I can't win this battle!"

Congratulations! You're right, you *can't* do this. You're powerless, but don't make the mistake of thinking that God is powerless. With supernatural intervention from God, you can leave the cycle of the curse and enjoy the cycle of the blessing. It doesn't matter what kind of battle you're facing; it could be alcoholism, a drug addiction, gambling, pornography, or any number of other things. What trips each of us up is temptation, so the real question is how to avoid taking the bait.

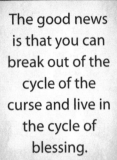

The good news is that you can break out of the cycle of the curse and live in the cycle of blessing.

The first step is to understand that taking the bait will *always* lead to suffering. You may be able to enjoy the sin or addiction for a while, but 100 percent of the time it will lead to incredible suffering. There are two things that drive people. One is seeking pleasure. The other is avoiding pain. No one in their right mind wants the kind of pain that will come when you take the bait. It's like getting hit over the head with a 2 x 4 with nails in it. You know it's going to hurt, but denial kicks in and you think, *It won't be so bad this time. I think I know how to handle it now. This time will be different.* If your brain could compute what the pain will be like in a few minutes, a few days, a few weeks, or even a year because of your choice, you wouldn't do it. Why? Because you want pleasure! Taking the bait will bring temporary pleasure followed by agonizing pain. You've got to learn to associate taking the bait with massive, massive amounts of pain.

Although it may be hard to resist taking the bait, recognize that gaining victory over it will put you in a place to receive revelation and intimacy with God. It will also put you on the fast track for the windows of heaven to open and pour out incredible blessings into your life. If you don't take the bait from the one who wants to destroy you, you'll move into a deeper relationship with the Living God.

Trust me, there's no high on earth or sin from hell that compares with the life, power, and destiny that He will infuse into your life. You've got to learn to associate *not* taking the bait with massive, massive amounts of pleasure, intimacy, and blessings.

The next step is to fall on your face and cry out to God. Get honest with Him; He knows the truth already—you're the only one who has been in denial. "God, this is a temptation that I've never been able to resist. For some reason, I keep taking the bait, and I've never been victorious over it. I'm begging You to help me resist this temptation. I beg You to save me and deliver me from all the schemes of the enemy." Pour your heart out to God, and let this be a step toward real honesty and intimacy with Him.

> There are two things that drive people. One is seeking pleasure. The other is avoiding pain.

The last and most important step is that you must meditate on God's Word day and night. Meditating means that you read God's Word, think on God's Word, and speak God's Word. The Hebrew word for *meditate* means "to mumble or to continuously talk out loud to yourself." This is a formula for success that is woven all the way through the Bible. After Moses died, when Joshua was about to lead the Israelites into the Promised Land, he faced overwhelming odds. For one thing, the city of Jericho was like a fortress surrounded with a wall thick enough that chariots could race across the top of it side by side. If that weren't bad enough, none of the people Joshua was leading had ever been in battle. The older generation who came out of Egypt had all died in the wilderness because they were afraid to fight the giants that lived in their Promised Land. They made a fatal mistake by saying something that God took great exception to. They said of the giants, "We are grasshoppers in their sight."

FACING YOUR GIANTS

The truth is that no matter what kind of battle you face, there are giants to be fought. The two biggest giants that are the root causes of all our problems are inferiority and insecurity. Satan's gateway to Eve's heart and to our hearts is the belief that "I'm not enough" (inferiority) and "If I'm not enough, I won't be loved" (insecurity). What defeats these giants is the truth of God's Word: "If God is for us, who can be against us? He who did not spare His own Son, but delivered Him up for us all, how shall He not with Him also freely give us all things?" (Romans 8:31–32). We are enough, and we loved.

> The Bible is a living Book, and it is the difference between victory and defeat. There is no other book on earth that is alive with God's power.

Each time you progress to the next level, there will be a giant to fight. Some of them are giant temptations, others are giant fears. Whatever giants stand between you and winning every battle, the same formula for success will work for you that worked for Joshua. It was God's secret to success for Joshua to take Jericho, defeat the giants, and win all his battles.

> *"This Book of the Law shall not depart from your mouth, but you shall meditate in it day and night, that you may observe to do according to all that is written in it. For then you will make your way prosperous, and then you will have good success. Have I not commanded you? Be strong and of good courage; do not be afraid, nor be dismayed, for the Lord your God is with you wherever you go."*
> JOSHUA 1:8–9 NKJV

Meditating on God's Word day and night will anchor your soul. It will empower you with strength from God. It will give you faith to win your battle. The Bible is a living Book, and it is the difference between victory and defeat. There is no other book on earth that is alive with God's power. As you spend time in it, God will start overhauling you from the inside out. He'll take out the sheetrock screws the enemy drove into your soul to tempt you to take the bait. He will take out old parts and put in new ones. In the Spirit, it sounds like a jackhammer breaking up the concrete around your heart. Before you know it, you'll have a new heart. You'll have a new way of thinking. You'll live in a new place of intimacy with God. Here's the best part: The bait won't look so good anymore. It won't have the power over you that it once held.

A PARADIGM SHIFT

Some people are never tempted by that bait again, others stumble and fall a few times, but whether you are instantly delivered or it happens over time, if you stay faithful in following these steps, there is no giant who can hold you down. Because under the old paradigm you had your eyes on the bait, and the temptation looked like a giant. It looked bigger than New York City. It looked bigger than God. But if you continue to meditate on God's Word day and night, your paradigm will shift. Your focus will shift from the temptation to God. Your vision will be corrected, and you'll see that the power of God is infinite and unable to be measured.

The tables will have been turned; you'll understand that God is the Giant, and your problem is the grasshopper. You won't even look at the bait, because your focus will be on God. It is from that intimacy with God that revelation flows, and it is that supernatural revelation that will cause you to win every battle.

When I met the man who tried to rob me of a half million dollars, the revelation God gave was simple. *"Don't say anything. Let Me handle this."* On other occasions, the revelation has been the next step toward victory. *"Call this person." "Go to that building." "Buy this land."*

Once I was sitting in the back of a room when God said, *"Mike, go start your own business."* Quicker than it will take me to write this, God downloaded the entire business plan to me.

With God, there are consequences to disobedience and blessings for obedience. The consequences of sin will be passed down to the third or fourth generation. However, the blessings of God will be passed down your generational line for 1,000 generations!

> *"I, the LORD your God, am a jealous God, punishing the children for the sin of the fathers to the third and fourth generation of those who hate me, but showing love to a thousand [generations] of those who love me and keep my commandments."*
> EXODUS 20:5–6

When you stop stumbling over obedience, you'll gain God's favor. When you gain God's favor, you'll enjoy God's blessings. For me, one of God's blessings came in the form of a 1922 Italian Renaissance Revival with an Italian Mediterranean tile roof and a sweet view of Milwaukee. That house was where our son, Michael, spoke his first words and took his first steps. It was more than a house; it was a home. It was a daily reminder of God's love, His patience, His favor, and His blessings.

> When you have nowhere else to turn, you're in the perfect place for a miracle. You are in the perfect position to win every battle.

I no longer live in Milwaukee, but when I think about that house, I realize afresh that when we come to the end of our own abilities, God hasn't even scratched the surface of His. When you have nowhere else to turn, you're in the perfect place for a miracle. You are in the perfect position to win every battle.

BATTLE PLAN

It's a mystery to most people why the measure of God's blessings seems to vary from person to person, and because of it God has gotten a bad rap. If you didn't understand the difference between love and favor, you might think that God was unfair. The truth is that God loves all of His children equally, but He doesn't favor them in equal measures. Love is a gift, but favor is earned through obedience. As an adult, I realized that my own choices to obey or disobey God's rules caused me to cycle in and out of His blessings. When you understand how to live in the blessings, you'll know how to win every battle.

BATTLE PRINCIPLES:

- Love is unconditional, but favor is earned by obedience.
- Obedience brings the favor of the Living God; the favor of God brings the blessings of God.
- There are cycles of blessings and cycles of the curse.
- Temptation is the stumbling block that determines if you will receive favor and blessings or discipline and suffering.
- Taking the bait will bring temporary pleasure followed by agonizing pain.
- When you shift your focus from the problem and onto God, the tables will have turned. God will be the Giant, and your problem will be the grasshopper.
- When you stop stumbling over obedience, you'll gain God's favor.
- When you gain God's favor, you will live in His blessings.

BATTLE STRATEGIES:

THE FIRST STEP: Associate with the Pain
Learn to associate taking the bait with massive, massive amounts of pain.

THE SECOND STEP: *Associate with the Pleasure*

Learn to associate not taking the bait with massive, massive amounts of pleasure, intimacy, and blessings.

THE THIRD STEP: *Cry out to God*

Fall on your face and cry out to God. Get honest with Him. He knows the truth already—you're the only one who has been in denial. "God, this is a temptation that I've never been able to resist. For some reason, I keep taking the bait, and I've never been victorious over it. I'm begging You to help me resist this temptation. I beg You to save me and deliver me from all the schemes of the enemy." Pour your heart out to God, and let this be a step toward real honesty and intimacy with Him.

THE FOURTH STEP: *Meditate on God's Word*

Meditate on God's Word day and night. Meditating means that you read God's Word, think on God's Word, speak God's Word, and mutter it to yourself. This is a formula for success that is woven all the way through the Bible. Meditating on God's Word day and night will anchor your soul. It will empower you with strength from God. It will give you faith to win your battle.

6

ANTI-DRIFT

Like most boys my age, there seemed to be a link between the production of testosterone and a love affair with cars. Girls would come later, but that first heady rush of adrenalin that made a guy faint with longing was sparked by the torque of an engine. By the age of 12, I had a fascination with cars. It wasn't enough to admire them as they roared past, although I did; I wanted to crawl under the hood and figure out all those moving parts. Long before I was a licensed driver, I knew my way around an engine and had learned to work on them. Back then, we didn't have electronic ignition or fuel injection; we had carburetors, points, and plugs. I learned to tune those babies until they roared to life, but no matter how well they'd been calibrated, over time they drifted out of calibration. Unlike cars today, if you didn't tune them up on a regular basis, you just might find yourself walking to the prom.

> **DRIFT**
> the certain, gradual erosion of standards and values.

Years later, I read a definition that made me think not only of those old cars, but of another key to winning every battle. According to the article I read, the definition of *drift* was, "the certain, gradual erosion of standards and values." Those early cars would drift off their calibration over time, and the same thing happens to individuals, companies, and whole societies.

I puzzled over that definition as I thought about my own journey to win every battle. I realized that we're a lot like those old cars. If we don't tune ourselves up and recalibrate daily, we'll drift off course. A very small drift may not seem like much, but by the end of your life, it might mean that you missed your destiny, which was God's best plan for you. Larger drifts off course could get you fired from your job or cooling your heels in prison. All sorts of bad things happen when we don't recalibrate ourselves to run in sync with our Maker.

ANTI-DRIFT™
the daily recalibration of standards and values.

In time, I trademarked another term—Anti-Drift™. Since I trademarked the term, I get to define it. Anti-Drift™ is the "daily recalibration of standards and values."

STAYING ON TRACK

How do you recalibrate in order to stay on track? Somehow you've got to get your finite self in sync with an infinite God. You've got to get to know Him in an intimate way. To do that, you've got to learn to hear His voice. It's staggering to me how many guys I know have never heard the voice of God.

"What do you mean you hear God?" my friends have asked, their voices raising a notch. They knew I wouldn't lie to them, so they believed me. "Man, you hear the voice of God. That's incredible!"

My response is, "It's actually more clear than audible."

Learning to hear the voice of God is crucial to winning every battle. How could you ever hope to win at war if you had no communication with your general? Yet millions of people go their whole lives—many of them Christians!—without ever hearing God's voice.

To me, that's a tragedy.

A lot of people think prayer is folding their hands, bowing their head, and then praying a prayer that goes out into space and never returns. That's why they live defeated lives; they don't think God cares enough to listen to or answer their prayers. Instead, they go from one defeat to another without ever hearing God's direction for their lives.

That's no way to live.

The Old Testament records that when God delivered the Israelites out of Egypt, He wanted a personal, intimate relationship with them. As a result, He invited them to meet with Him on Mount Sinai. They missed their opportunity because they were *afraid*. Many of the people I talk to won't go into the closet to meet the Living God for the very reason that they're afraid of Him. If they only knew—being in a closet or in any intimate relationship with God is the safest place on earth!

THE POWER OF PRAYER

Prayer is communication between you and God. You speak; God answers. God speaks; you answer. God's definition of prayer involves talking, listening, sharing, fellowship, intimacy, guidance, direction, protection, provision, and power. It's dangerous to go through life without asking and receiving guidance from God.

Why is it so hard for people—especially men—to hear God's voice? The first reason is that many people have never been taught that it was possible, and they've never been taught how to position themselves to hear. The second reason involves the busyness of our lives and the constant bombarding of noise and thoughts that speeds like a NASCAR race through our minds at any given moment in time.

If men were cars, most of us would run at 10,000 revolutions per minute. That's the way we were wired. With your mind racing at that speed, it's next to impossible to hear God's voice. He's speaking on a different frequency, and in order to hear Him we must slow down to 500 revolutions per minute. That's why the Bible tells us to, "Be still and know that I am God." We have to slow down and get still in order to know God.

SHIFTING INTO LOW GEAR

Do you remember the first time you fell in love? Sure you do. It's unforgettable. Perhaps you were in fourth grade, or a senior in college, or walking down an aisle at a business trade show. For most guys, it typically works like this. You looked up and saw "her," and everything going on around you disappeared as she was freeze-framed in the movie of your life. You felt your knees get weak, and your heart pounded so hard you could hear its echo in your ears. In that moment, nothing else mattered. The only coherent thought you could form was that somehow you had to get to know her.

But in order to get to know her, you had to slow down. You had to make getting to know her your priority rather than just being consumed by that strong instinctive attraction you felt. You had to let other things go so you could find out if she was truly the person you hoped she was. When you spent time with her, you focused on her. You watched her face and listened intently to every word she said. You learned what she liked, and what she didn't like. You discovered her values, and what she believed. You figured out what made her eyes light with laughter.

When you move from falling in love to being in love, you shift into slow gear.

INTIMACY WITH GOD

Getting to know God in an intimate way is very much the same. The first step has to be the decision, *I have to know Him!* If you make the further decision to know Him, to know more of Him, you'll experience a dimension of life you didn't know possible. The second step is to make spending time with Him a high priority, even if it means letting other things go. The third step is slowing down all the mind traffic so you can hear His voice.

If you were going to approach a king, queen, or a president, you would follow careful protocols. So how do you approach the King of all kings? According to Psalm 100:4 (NASB), we are to, "Enter into his gates with thanksgiving, and into his courts with praise: give thanks unto him, and bless his name." The Bible says that God inhabits the praise of His people.

The first thing I do when I want an audience with God is to turn on praise music and worship Him. Depending on where I am and what's going on, I may play the music through the speakers in my house. Sometimes I get alone and put on my Bose headphones. When I'm traveling, I always take my iPod that is filled with praise music. In addition to praise ushering us into God's presence, I believe that angels are drawn to praise to God, and I want them around me and my family with their swords drawn.

The next step in the process is crucial, and if you're a man, your reaction to it may have been as negative as mine was when God instructed me to do it. The next step is journaling. I know! I know! It sounds feminine, and I moaned and groaned about it too—but it catapulted me into a whole new level with God. We all need this step if we're going to win every battle. This is what separates the Rangers and the Green Beret Special Forces from the Boy Scout Tenderfoots in the battle. Get this right and you will become a paratrooper for the Living God. You won't have fear, but you'll have purpose, meaning, and courage.

A better term for journaling is, "Talking and listening to the Living God." When you first begin this process, try writing a few sentences of praise to Him and then write a few thanking Him for His goodness. I added a few lines of what I was thinking. In order to do this I had to slow down so I could listen and think. A week later I heard or felt the Voice. It was the Living God speaking and fellow-shipping directly with me. It was unbelievable.

When you're going to start something you're not thrilled to be doing, I suggest handling it as though you were cleaning out a closet. Most people are stuck saving things we *might* need sometime in the future. We "what if..." ourselves until we have a closet filled with junk. My tip for cleaning out a closet is that you limit yourself to re-moving only one thing a day. Under no circumstances should you remove more than one item per day. The result is that you want to take more out of the closet. The stuff you once thought about sav-ing is now relegated to the trash bin.

Likewise, I recommend that when you start journaling, you limit yourself to three minutes a day for the first week. Under no circum-stances should you go a second past three minutes. Let me tell you what will happen: it's going to hurt to put your pen down and walk away. During the second week, you increase your time journaling to six minutes—but not seven. Eventually you'll get up to 20 or 30 min-utes, and then you're on your own. You'll never stop.

JOURNALING 101

I keep a journal or notebook with me, and once I praise my way into the Lord's presence, I start to write. My first attempts looked something like this.

Oh, man, I'm really dreading this, but God You know I love You. What else can I say? I'm kind of dry here. I'm out. I don't think I have anything else. I'm done. I really don't know what to say. Oh yeah! I just remembered the time You bailed my hind end out of that deal that was heading toward a new episode on the Sopranos. I'll never forget that. You got me out of that mess alive and with all my body parts, not to mention the money they owed me! I'm not sure that I ever thanked You enough for that one. So...that's it.

Wait a minute, there was the time I was driving through heavy traffic and You guided me—I still don't know how You did it—and I knew that I should turn left instead of right. If I'd gone right, I would be dead right now. We'd be talking about this in person. So I just wanted to say thank You for saving me that time too.

Hey, remember that time on Northwest Expressway when I was driving at night and You made me changes lanes at a stoplight? I obeyed, and at the last second a drunk came roaring through and totaled the car where mine had been sitting. I didn't really know how to hear Your voice, but the message was so strong I got it. When I think about all the ways You've rescued me...

When you do that, eventually you'll hear the Lord answer. Just write it down. You can go five minutes, ten minutes, or longer. There have been a few occasions when I received something like a laser beam, high velocity download from heaven into my brain and onto the paper...page after page...stopping only because I was too exhausted to continue writing. It was *incredible*.

HEARING GOD'S VOICE

There are several ways we hear God's voice. First, we often hear God speak to us through a pastor or another person. We also hear God's voice through the Bible; the whole Book is God speaking to us and teaching us His ways. In addition, on rare occasions, we might hear God speak audibly. God also speaks to our hearts, as I just described. There is a check and balance system for all of these ways of hearing. We need that check and balance system because our mind filters our own voice, the voice of the world, and the voice of the enemy.

So how do you know that what you're hearing is from God? First and foremost, remember that God will never speak anything that disagrees with or opposes the Bible; it is the standard by which everything is measured. For that reason, it's imperative that you spend time reading and meditating on the Bible, because by doing so you will learn God's voice and His will. The entire Bible is God's general will for your life; what you hear in your private prayer time is His specific will for your life. If you hear something that is major, life changing, or that you question, take what you heard to someone in spiritual authority over your life and ask them to pray over it, either confirming or denying that it is God's will for your life.

Often the Lord will tell you things to come before they occur. Sometimes He will give you wisdom from heaven that will cause you to win your battle. Another great way to check what you're hearing is by going back and reading what you heard weeks, months, or even a year before. If you're in sync with God, you'll be astounded at how many of those things will have come to pass.

TRANSCEIVERS

In talk radio, there are transmitters and receivers. The transmitters transmit a signal, and the receiver receives it. There are also transceivers, which both transmit and receive. When we are in proper sync with the Living God, we are transceivers, because the communication is flowing back and forth in both directions. That's the way God created us to relate to Him. The sad truth is that the vast majority of Christians are transmitters only; they pray but don't know how to receive from God. Life is too short to live without supernatural intervention from our Creator.

When God first told me to journal, He said, "Mike, I want you to do this for 30 days." Still grousing, I took my trash can down our long concrete drive to the curb. "God, I don't want to get hit by lightning or anything, so I am asking you this in all humility. Why do I need to journal for 30 straight days?"

Bam! The answer came out of nowhere like a fastball, the message intense and crystal clear. *"Because it takes 30 days to make a habit, and you're going to be doing this for the rest of your life."*

Today I can't imagine living life without that daily intimacy with God. I couldn't stand to go a week without hearing His voice and journaling what He tells me. This is the kind of prayer that brings heaven down to earth. It is in those times alone with God that He teaches me, changes me, and fills me with more of Himself. It is there that God downloads the battle plans and strategies for the wars ahead. There's nothing feminine about it; it's like going to the War Room and meeting with the Commander and Chief.

During war time, one of the primary strategies is to knock out the enemy's communication system. If you can stop your enemy's communication, you can win the war. That's the reason so many Christians live defeated lives; the enemy has convinced them that they can't hear the voice of God. Each and every day of your life the Commander and Chief is in the War Room, waiting to meet with you. If you want to win every battle, I suggest you keep that appointment.

BATTLE PLAN

We're a lot like the old cars I loved as a kid. If we aren't re-calibrated daily, we'll drift off course and end up somewhere we don't want to be. Anti-Drift™ is the daily recalibration of our standards and values. God created us, and He offers full service maintenance and beyond—it's a Lifetime Platinum Guarantee. His Anti-Drift™ Plan includes time spent in His presence each day while He recalibrates us. Part of that process involves learning to hear God's voice. You can't win a war without a battle plan, and you won't get your battle plan without meeting God in the War Room.

BATTLE PRINCIPLES:

- Learning to hear the voice of God is crucial to winning every battle. How could you ever hope to win at war if you had no communication with your general?

- Prayer is communication between you and God. You speak; God answers. God's definition of prayer involves talking, listening, sharing, fellowship, intimacy, guidance, direction, protection, provision, and power.

- It's dangerous to go through life without asking and receiving guidance from God.

- God speaks on a different frequency. We have to slow down and get still in order to know God.

- God speaks to us through the Bible and through other people. He speaks to our hearts and on rare occasions He speaks audibly.

- Our minds filter our own voice, the voice of the world, and the voice of the enemy. That's why it's important that we have a system of checks and balances.

- It's imperative that you spend time reading and meditating on the Bible, because by doing so you will learn God's voice and His will.

BATTLE STRATEGIES:

THE FIRST STEP: The Decision
The first step has to be the decision, *I must know Him!*

THE SECOND STEP: Setting Your Priorities
The second step is to make spending time with God a high priority.

THE THIRD STEP: Slow Down
We live in a world where we are bombarded with information, thoughts, noise, and so much mind traffic that to God our heads must sound like a NASCAR race. In order to hear God's voice, we've got to slow down and *listen*.

THE FOURTH STEP: Enter His Gates
There are protocols for approaching royalty. According to the Bible, praise and thanksgiving will open the gates to God's court and usher us into His presence. I begin my prayer time with praise music, thanking Him and worshipping my way into His presence. I travel with praise music on my iPod that I listen to on the airplane.

THE FIFTH STEP: Journal
Once I praise my way into God's presence, I journal all my thanks to Him in a free-flowing, comfortable way. As I listen, God speaks, and I write what I hear. This is a powerful form of Anti-Drift™, because it is in God's presence that He recalibrates us and keeps us on course for victory.

THE SIXTH STEP: Checks and Balances
God will never speak anything to you that is in opposition to

the Bible. The written Word of God is the standard by which everything is measured. If you hear something life changing or anything that you question, take what you heard and submit it to someone in spiritual authority and ask them to pray over it for clarity.

THE SEVENTH STEP: Stay in the Word of God

The entire Bible is God's general will for your life; what you hear in your private prayer time is His specific will for your life. If you read and meditate on the Bible each day, you'll learn to hear God's voice and His will through the written Word.

THE EIGHTH STEP: Journal Every Day for 30 Days

It takes 30 days to form a new habit, and you will be doing this for the rest of your life. When you learn to meet the Commander and Chief in the War Room and receive His battle plan, you will win every battle.

7

THE WONDER OF WORDS

"**T**hat guy's going to end up in prison and take us with him!" I said as I slammed the back door and stomped snow off my shoes.

Dana looked up from the stove, where the scent of something delicious wafted through the house. "Mike, you've *got* to stop saying things like that," she said, a determined look on her face.

Oh, brother. Here we go again, I thought. This argument had been simmering for months, and I saw no resolution in sight. None of what she said made sense to me.

"Look," I said, "I just call things as I see them. That old saying that business makes strange bedfellows is true. You don't really know what a person is made of until there's a lot of money at stake. I'm telling you the truth, and you'd better listen to me: Something's not right! I don't know what it is, but something is so rotten in this deal that I can smell it. You used to trust my business instincts; what happened?"

"Mike, we've been over this a hundred times. I *do* trust your instincts. I don't think that you're wrong in your assessment of the situation, just in what you say about it."

"Oh, for heaven's sake, I'm just telling what's going on."

"No, you're cursing him, and you're cursing us!"

"What are you talking about?"

"You *said* that he would end up in prison. And then you *said* that he would take us with him. I don't want you to speak those things over him or over us, because there is power in your words and you can cause it to happen! If you want a different outcome, you'd better start blessing him and the situation."

"Are you *kidding me?* This guy's a shark, and I'm his bait!"

Dana walked out of the kitchen and went upstairs.

"*What?*" I called after her.

THE POWER OF THE TONGUE

I didn't understand what she was talking about, but I thought that any day now she would come to her senses and let me off the hook. But for a full year, she stopped me every time I said anything that she considered negative. Meanwhile, the man I was doing a business deal with in another state continued to lie, cheat, and steal. Did I have any proof? No, but I felt sure that he was operating outside the law, and as his partner, I might be liable.

"But it's the *truth!*" I argued months later. "It might be better for all of us if a truck hit him!"

"*Mike!* Just *listen* to yourself! What you speak over him will come back on you!"

To say I didn't get it would be an understatement. But one day, I can't even tell you when it happened, it was like someone flipped a switch. I *got it!* My thought process went something like this. *Oh, man! My words have power! I don't like what I'm seeing in this situation, so I'm going to change what I say! I'm going to speak blessings!*

The next time something came up with that out-of-state partner who was up to no good, I prayed with a different attitude. "God, as Your servant, I command Your richest blessings over this man and over his wife and children. I pray that Your blessings would overtake him and that he would be blessed in a way that he has never known. I ask that your blessings would cause all the strategies of the enemy that have been set against him to fall before the mighty name of Jesus."

Every time something happened that made me want to grit my teeth, I blessed him instead. I blessed his health. I blessed his children. I blessed his business. I blessed his finances. The strangest thing started happening. A new measure of God's blessings began pouring over me, my health, my son, my business, and my finances.

Weeks later, the man asked to meet with me. "We've got a problem," he said.

"What's that?" I asked.

"I haven't been honest with you," he admitted. "I've lied to you from the beginning of this deal, but I can't keep up the charade. I want you to know that I'll make it right."

"I forgive you," I said. He seemed taken aback by my quick forgiveness and lack of anger. Looking back, I realized that it had been God alerting me to the problem, but my reaction had been wrong, and my words had tied His hands. Although we're still walking out the solution to the problem he created, I now understand that we had both been duped by the enemy.

YOU HAVE CREATIVE POWER

Here's what was happening. Not only had I been speaking wrong words over his life—they were bouncing back on mine! Why? It's a spiritual principle. Whatever you plant, you will harvest. If you plant negative things with your words, you will reap a negative harvest. When your harvest is ripe and negativity fills your storehouse, you look around at others who are being blessed with good things and think, *I wonder why God is blessing them and He isn't blessing me?*

We choose our harvest by what we plant. It works the same way whether we speak negative or positive words. We can have what we say. It doesn't happen overnight. If you planted a vegetable garden, it would take time for the seeds to sprout and grow, and the same is true with your words.

> Your life today is a picture of what you have believed and spoken in the past.

Take a good, hard look at your life. Notice all the good things; and notice all the bad things. Your life today is a picture of what you have believed and spoken in the past.

If you don't like what you see in your life right now, don't be discouraged because you can change it. God allows each of us to be the prophet of our own life. By that I mean we have the authority to speak into existence the life and outcome we desire. So if you're in a battle today, what have you spoken over it? Have you spoken defeat? Have you spoken great victory?

Words are one of the most powerful components to winning every battle, and one of the sneakiest ways we are often defeated. This is where almost everyone stumbles into defeat. To some degree or another we all have been trapped by our own words. Professionals, pastors, ministers, and prophets all fall into this sneakiest of all sneak attacks. By the words of our own mouths, we are snared.

MADE IN GOD'S IMAGE

You may be wondering how this works, and that's a fair question. Depending on where you live, if you stepped out of your home or office right now, you might see green pastures, trees, and flowers in riotous colors. You might see desert or the lapping waters of a lake. You might see snow-tipped mountains or fields ripe with wheat. No matter where you live or what you see, the earth and all of its fullness was created by God.

God didn't just create the earth, but the entire universe. The Bible says that He measured the foundation of the world with His hands. He set the sun in its place. He formed every star and all the galaxies. God didn't mold a star in His hand. He created everything that is out of nothing that was.

He *spoke* them into being.

> **God spoke the world into existence.**

The Bible describes creation. "In the beginning God created the heavens and the earth. Now the earth was formless and empty, darkness was over the surface of the deep, and the Spirit of God was hovering over the waters. And God *said*, 'Let there be light,' and there was light" (Genesis 1:1–3, emphasis mine).

God spoke everything into existence. He spoke the sky, the dry earth, the seas, night, day, the sun, the moon and all living creatures into being.

Then God said, "Let us make man in our image, in our likeness, and let them rule over the fish of the sea and the birds of the air, over the livestock, over all the earth, and over all the creatures that move along the ground."

So God created man in his own image, in the image of God he created him; male and female he created them.

ABRAHAM'S MIRACLE

God created everything in every galaxy by the words that He spoke. Then He created us in His own image. Like God, creative power resides in the words we speak. There is creative power wrapped around each of our words that calls into being whatever we say.

One of the best examples of this in the Bible is the story of Abram. God chose to have a relationship with Abram out of all the people on earth. God blessed him and caused him to prosper and become very rich. There was one major problem though. Abram had no children. The story unfolds in Genesis 15:2–6.

> *But Abram said, "O Sovereign LORD, what can you give me since I remain childless and the one who will inherit my estate is Eliezer of Damascus?" And Abram said, "You have given me no children; so a servant in my household will be my heir." Then the word of the LORD came to him: "This man will not be your heir, but a son coming from your own body will be your heir." He took him outside and said, "Look up at the heavens and count the stars—if indeed you can count them." Then he said to him, "So shall your offspring be." Abram believed the LORD, and he credited it to him as righteousness.*

Abram believed God, which is amazing, because nothing happened. Years passed, and he still had no children. At this point, most of us would have been murmuring and complaining that God didn't keep His word.

When Abram was *99 years old*, God spoke to him again about having a son.

> *When Abram was ninety-nine years old, the LORD appeared to him and said, "I am God Almighty; walk before me and be blameless. I will confirm my covenant between me and you and will greatly increase your numbers." Abram fell facedown, and God said to him, "As for me, this is my covenant with you: You will be the father of many nations. No longer will you be called Abram; your name will be Abraham, for I have made you a father of many nations. I will make you very fruitful; I will make nations of you, and kings will come from you."*
> GENESIS 17:1–6

ABRAHAM'S SON

When Abram reached the ripe old age of 99, God changed his name to Abraham, which means "Father of Many Nations." Every time he met someone he said, "Hello, I'm the Father of Many Nations." Each time someone called his name they said, "Hey, Father of Many Nations!" God got Abraham's creative words, activating the promise and calling it into existence.

In Romans 4:19, the Bible says that Abraham's body was as good as dead and that Sarah's womb *was* dead. Yet at the age of 100, Abraham impregnated his wife, and Sarah bore him a son. In order for Abraham to win his battle for children, he had to speak what God said about him. In Romans 4:17, the Bible says that He called those things that did not exist into existence.

> God got Abraham's creative words activating the promise and calling it into existence.

Many of us have spent our lives calling things as we see them instead of calling those things that do not exist into existence. I believe the enemy has worked hard to blind us to the creative power of our words.

Our words will call into existence those things that we speak, either positive or negative. One of the saddest examples of this in the Bible occurred after God brought the Israelites out of Egypt. These were the same people who had crossed the Red Sea on dry ground while God held the water back on either side of them. They drank water that God caused to flow from a rock. They ate manna. Their shoes and clothes never wore out.

In other words, they experienced miracles that most of the world could only dream about. God led them by a pillar of fire at night and a cloud by day. He brought them out of Egypt and was personally escorting them to the Promised Land.

Yet only two of that original group lived to see that land of promise.

How in the world could you be defeated if God was fighting for you?

THEY GOT WHAT THEY SAID

They stumbled over their own tongues, while the devil and his cohorts laughed. The Bible says that they sinned by murmuring and complaining. I know, it doesn't seem like much of a sin to us, does it? Yet murmuring and complaining is off God's Richter scale of sins. Why? They used their creative power to agree with the enemy instead of with God.

Over and over throughout their journey, they prophesied their own demise. They whined, "We will die in this wilderness!" They continued saying that after God parted the Red Sea. They whined the same words about the manna. They complained about everything by saying, "We will die in this wilderness!"

Finally, after refusing to believe that God could lead them to victory against the giants in the land, they wailed, "We will die in this wilderness!" There followed one of the saddest verses in the Bible.

"'As I live,' says the LORD, 'just as you have spoken in My hearing, so I will do to you'" (Numbers 14:28 NKJV).

Except for Joshua and Caleb, who spoke the will of the Lord, they all died in the wilderness. It wasn't God's plan, but they called it into existence with the power of their words. You and I have the same power in our words today.

BLESS YOUR CHILDREN

Every parent needs to grasp that they are creating in their children whatever it is that they say about them. I heard a mother whose son went to prison say, "I told that boy every day of his life that he was going to end up in prison. Did he listen to me?"

Yes, he did. Not only that, but God listened. The enemy who

wanted him to end up in prison was listening. Of course, you have to deal with your children's mistakes and wrong choices, but you have an audience waiting to hear what you say over your children's life. Just like my business partner, they need you to bless them, not curse them.

Even though it took me years to learn how to use my words to bring about victory in business, I had an instinct to protect my son from negative words. For instance, unless I'm out of town, I drive him to school every morning. Instead of getting in line behind the other cars that circle through the drive and drop their children off at the door, I chose to make use of that time with my son. I park the car and walk with him. Along the way, we stop, and I put my hand on his head and speak a blessing over him.

> Like us, our children need our blessings the most when they deserve them the least.

"Heavenly Father," I pray, "please assign Your angels to guard and protect Michael. I ask that they have their swords out to defend him. May You cause Michael to have ears to hear Your voice and a heart that obeys You."

One day I looked at him and said, "Michael, do you realize that God made you perfect?"

Michael is nine, and he knows that he makes his share of mistakes. But that morning he looked up at me in awe. "You mean I'm good?" he asked, his entire being on high alert. He almost held his breath, quivering in anticipation of my answer.

"Yes, you are," I said. "You're the perfect son. I'm so happy to be your dad." Those words were alive as they touched my son.

I have a question that I ask my son, and I have trained him how to answer.

"Who can take this blessing from you, my son?" I ask.

"No man can take this blessing from me," he responds.

Once the blessings we speak are received, they release supernatural power.

MIRACLES IN YOUR MOUTH

Life is filled with hard knocks, even for our children. We need to bathe them in blessings. Like us, they may need our blessings the most when they deserve them the least. That's the heart of the Gospel, you know. While we were still sinners, Christ died for us. God poured out the greatest blessing heaven had to offer when we deserved the worst. I am so grateful to God that He didn't look at me and call things as He saw them. He looked at me and called things into existence that had not existed.

That's the creative miracle we can offer people in our world each day.

Of all the sneaky, underhanded, and cruel schemes of the enemy, I think the lowest and most underhanded is ensnaring us into defeat by our own words.

Imagine that the battle that you're facing was a ball game. Your own negative self-talk causes you to think and say, "I'm going to be struck out." "That pitcher is too fast for me." "I'm not fast enough." "I'm not smart enough." "I'm not strong enough." "The bases are loaded, and I don't have a chance."

Allow yourself to get a revelation of who you are. In Christ, you're Babe Ruth! The bases are loaded, and the score is tied. The people in the stands are silent, because you're up to bat. You point to center field and say, "The ball will not go by me. I won't be struck out. I'm going to hit this ball out of the ballpark. It's going over the fence. It's going into the parking lot and through someone's windshield. This is a home run, because God is on my side and He gave me the words to say that cause it to come to pass."

You will make a home run, because you spoke the end from the beginning.

You can win every battle.

There are miracles in your mouth.

BATTLE PLAN

Of all the principles in this book, this is the one where most of us are defeated. As we go about our day, the world lulls us into a false sense of complacency about what we say; it's easy to talk like everyone else and spin tales about how bad things have gotten. The enemy also works hard at blinding us to the creative power that is in our words. In the heat of a battle, fear and anxiety attempt to squeeze us until we speak what the enemy is saying about our situation instead of what God has said about our victory.

Proverbs 18:21 says it best, "Death and life are in the power of the tongue; and they that love it shall eat the fruit thereof" (ASV). There are miracles in our mouth. Defeat also resides there. Every day of our lives, every time we open our mouth to speak, we make a choice to speak life and blessing or death and cursing.

The Bible is filled with warnings about what we say, but one of the strongest admonitions is found in James 3:1–10 (LB):

"If anyone can control his tongue, it proves that he has perfect control over himself in every other way. We can make a large horse turn around and go wherever we want by means of a small bit in his mouth. And a tiny rudder makes a huge ship turn wherever the pilot wants it to go, even though the winds are strong. So also the tongue is a small thing, but what enormous damage it can do. A great forest can be set on fire by one tiny spark. And the tongue is a flame of fire. It is full of wickedness, and poisons every part of the body. And the tongue is set on fire by hell itself, and can turn our whole lives into a blazing flame of destruction and disaster. Men have trained, or can train, every kind of animal or bird that lives and every kind of reptile and fish, but no human being can tame the tongue. It is always ready to pour out its deadly poison. Sometimes it praises our heavenly Father, and sometimes it breaks out into curses against men who are made like God. And so blessing and cursing come pouring out of the same mouth. Dear brothers, surely this is not right!"

If you want to win every battle, you've first got to win the war over your tongue.

BATTLE PRINCIPLES:

■ God spoke the world into existence, and we are made in His image. Creative power resides in our words.

■ There are miracles in your mouth.

■ Your life today is a picture of what you have believed and spoken in the past.

■ You have the authority to speak into existence the life and outcome you desire.

■ Words are one of the most powerful components to winning every battle, and one of the sneakiest ways we are often defeated.

■ In order for Abraham to win his battle for children, he had to speak what God said about him. In Romans 4:17, the Bible says that He called those things that did not exist into existence.

■ We have been blinded to the creative power of our words. Our words will call into existence those things we speak, either positive or negative.

■ "'As I live,' says the LORD, 'just as you have spoken in My hearing, so I will do to you'" (Numbers 14:28 NKJV).

■ Like all of us, our children need our blessings most when they deserve them the least.

■ We can speak creative miracles over people in our world each day.

BATTLE STRATEGIES:

THE FIRST STEP: Know the Truth

We're a lot like Superman before he knew that kryptonite would strip him of his supernatural power. If you're like me, for most of my life I didn't realize there was a miracle in my mouth. The first step to winning the war over your tongue is to get settled in your heart that you can have what you say. If you're still not sure, all you have to do is study the Bible on the subject. You'll be stunned to see that it's a recurring theme.

THE SECOND STEP: *Breaking the Habit*

Most of us have spent our lives being programmed to call it as we see it. The pull of speaking negative things is so great that most of the time we don't even hear ourselves doing it. Practice saying what you want instead of what you have!

THE THIRD STEP: *Stop Rehearsing the Problem*

Don't rehearse your faults. Instead, confess them to God and repent. Don't rehearse the problems in business, in your personal life, or in your children's lives. Don't rehearse your spouse's problems. Speak victory over every situation in your life. In order to do that, you'll need to stop the negative thoughts. When your mind is filled with negative images, switch channels. Force yourself to picture and speak the victory you desire.

THE FOURTH STEP: *A Little Help from a Friend*

Negative words are so ingrained in us that most of us don't hear ourselves speaking defeat. Although I didn't realize it at first, one of the things that helped me most was being confronted with the negative things I said. Talk this over with your close circle of friends and ask them for help. Agree on an easy, nonthreatening way to point out the problem without pointing a finger.

THE FIFTH STEP: *Never, Ever Quit*

No matter how much progress you've made in using the creative power of your words, you can never let down your guard, because the world will lull you to sleep to the miracle in our mouth. If you're going to win every battle, make a quality decision that you'll never, ever quit. Abraham was 100 years old before he experienced his miracle and held Isaac in his arms. No matter what your situation, it's never too late, and you're never too old to win the war over your words.

8

THE STRENGTH OF COVENANT

My heart ricocheted off my chest like machine gun fire; my hands felt clammy as I stood in the courtroom feeling more like I faced a firing squad than an appellate court. It was the second semester of my first year in law school, and the appellate advocacy class was my first experience at anything close to practicing real law. The competition was stiff, the classes were hard, and I had made a C in each of the five classes during the first semester, a less than stellar start.

Like most first-year law students, I'd heard horror stories about the appellate class. Each of us had to write and argue an appellate brief before mock judges. It doesn't sound so bad, does it? After all, it was a mock trial, and no real plaintiff was going to lose a case based on how we did. All that hung in the balance was our law careers, our grades, and how we were perceived by the faculty. It would be a trial by fire. The judges included one of the most brilliant professors in law and two of the most brilliant upperclassmen in the law school. Their entire job was to break us, demean us, tear us to shreds, and feed us to the dogs. It was a no-holes-barred attack on what we were supposed to have learned, and also on whatever vestige of self-esteem had survived first semester.

Although I didn't usually pray about my grades, I prayed for an A in this class, which in view of my first semester grades was about as likely as my being the first matriculating law student appointed to the Supreme Court of the United States. "This class is about the real practice of law," I explained to the Lord. "I'll do all the work. I'm not trying to slough off. But I'm asking you to give me an A, and I'm dedicating this class to you."

> *Castleberry v. State.* The words dropped into my mind from nowhere. Where had that come from?

I had prepared my brief and studied until it felt like my brain had gone up in smoke. It was as if I could hear Scotty, the engineer of the Starship Enterprise, talking about my brain and yelling at Captain Kirk, "The engines can't take anymore, Captain—they're gonna blow!"

Now that I was here in the courtroom, I felt as unprepared as a freshman trying to take the Bar Exam. My opponent, a gifted female student, had 15 minutes to argue her case, and after she finished I would have my 15 minutes in the flame. She was only five minutes into her argument and the judges had pounded her without mercy. *O Lord,* I thought as I fumbled to review my notes for the 10 minutes remaining.

Castleberry v. State. The words dropped into my mind from nowhere. Where had that come from? I swatted the thought away like a pesky fly and focused on my notes.

Castleberry v. State. The thought came back, buzzing me like a mosquito. I shook it off, trying to prepare myself while witnessing my fellow student's massacre. It was worse than a train wreck; I felt like a voyeur watching someone's suffering, and I knew that within a matter of minutes they would tear into me. My hands shook as I turned a page.

I looked at the clock. She had one minute left.

"Castleberry v. State!" This time it sounded like someone screamed in my ear. My whole body heard the words.

Oh, my God! It's the Voice! I had been meticulous about briefing all the cases pertinent to the appeal, and I'd alphabetized them. With what seemed like hundreds of briefs in front of me, I turned to Castleberry v. State. I read the one-page brief, and the second I finished the last word, the judges called me to the front of the courtroom. Every molecule of my being shook as I approached the lectern.

WINNING EVERY BATTLE

"Counselor Galiga, what can you tell us about..."

The two upperclassmen fired questions at me like bullets—fifty caliber bullets—each one light years harder and with more force than the one before. Their job was to find my breaking point and snap me. I held my own, but what made my knees buckle was not what the law professor did but what he didn't do. Not only had he not asked me a single question, he hadn't even looked up at me. Not once. I knew the strategy; he was going to wait until the last minute and go for my jugular. It was a merciless move. No one had a chance against him.

I was 14 minutes into my arguments with only one minute to go when the professor looked up at me. This, I knew, was going to be the atomic bomb of all questions. It would be the question that no person from earth could ever answer. I felt faint. I was so exhausted that I couldn't have answered the question, "What is your name, Michael Galiga?" I had nothing left. I'd given all I had, but now the professor was circling me like a predator about to go in for the kill.

"Counselor," he began, "how would you differentiate the case before us..." he paused for effect, "from Castleberry v. State?"

It felt like an electric shock rippled through my body. When the professor looked at me, all he saw was a clueless first-year law student. He had no idea that the Supreme Judge of all judges had whispered that case in my ear. Further, He caused the smartest man I'd ever met to ask me the question He wanted asked. I wanted to shout! Instead, with all the dignity I could muster, I told him the minutest details about Castleberry v. State, details even he would have had to look up and a supercomputer would have had difficulty compiling.

You could feel the shock waves crash like a riptide through the courtroom and onto all three judges. The other two judges had prepared me for this crucifixion, as they had all the others. The professor looked at me in complete astonishment. He was flabbergasted. I could see what he was thinking as though it were a neon sign on his forehead, *If he could answer this question, he could answer any question.* It was over; he was finished with me.

"Counselor," he said, "you obviously cannot be broken."

I could hardly believe my ears. He asked the *only* question for which I had the answer. The only one!

That professor was the most brilliant man I'd ever met, and he still holds that distinction today. Because I knew the answers to Castleberry v. State, he thought *I* was brilliant. From that moment on, he treated me with utmost respect. Needless to say, I got an A.

THE POWER OF PROMISE

All these years later, I still can't think about Castleberry v. State without an overwhelming sense of awe. God knew that was the atom bomb designed to blow me into a mushroom cloud. It would be years before I learned that I could live with that kind of divine intervention every day of my life. So why did He tip me off to the answer I would need?

The answer is simple: I was in covenant with Him, and I asked.

When I was in high school and I gave my life to Jesus, at that moment God became my covenant partner. It didn't matter that I knew nothing about being in covenant; God knew, and He did His part.

Covenant isn't a word that has much meaning in modern America. Judges and lawyers may understand it better than anyone because a covenant is legally binding. For example, a covenant could be a contractual agreement between two parties. In both God's law and in man's law, a covenant isn't something to be taken lightly.

In its simplest form, a covenant is a promise between two people.

Native American tribes understood covenants, although they called them peace treaties. On occasion, two tribes would make a peace treaty that involved a ceremony where they mingled their blood, making them as though they were one tribe. The covenant, or treaty, couldn't be broken. Afterward, if one of the tribes was attacked, the tribe they were in covenant with was obligated to defend them. In covenant, the stronger partner always is obligated to defend the weaker partner.

> In both God's law and in man's law, a covenant isn't something to be taken lightly.

If men know how to make and honor a covenant relationship, can you imagine what infinite resources are available when we're in covenant with the Living God? In my case, the weaker partner—me—called out to the stronger partner—God—and asked for help with my advocacy class. In response to my request, God instructed me to read Castleberry v. State. There is *nothing* better than being in covenant with God.

To better understand covenants, we'll go back in time to when God made a covenant with Abraham. God promised Abraham a son and said that through him the whole world would be blessed. When he was 100 years old, Abraham's son Isaac was born. One of Isaac's descendants was Jesus, who offered Himself as the ultimate sacrifice for our sins. No one in the history of mankind has blessed the world as Jesus did.

Abraham's descendants through Isaac became Israel, the people we know as Jews. Some Christians believe what's called the "replacement theory," which says that God's covenant with the Jews was replaced with His covenant with the Church. God cannot lie and will not break covenant; therefore His covenant with Abraham's descendents still stands. They are God's chosen people and will always be God's chosen people.

GRAFTED INTO THE OLIVE TREE

However, this replacement theology is, in part, what has robbed the Church of its power. All you have to do is read the New Testament to see that the early Church operated in great power with signs, miracles, and wonders. Not only did they heal the sick, they preached the Gospel and 3,000 people were added to the Church in a single day. What happened? While we do still see signs, wonders, and miracles, they are rare by anyone's standard, and the Church as a whole doesn't experience them. However, when people who are properly aligned to the Living God and understand their authority in Christ speak, this same power is released.

> In covenant, the stronger partner always is obligated to defend the weaker partner.

The explanation of the problem of powerlessness is found in the Bible. In Romans 11:17–27, God made our relationship with Israel clear. Yes, Israel. He likened the Jews to an olive tree and said that we, the Christ followers, were grafted into it.

If some of the branches have been broken off, and you, though a wild olive shoot, have been grafted in among the others and now share in the nourishing sap from the olive root, do not boast over those branches. If you do, consider this: You do not support the root, but the root supports you. You will say then, "Branches were broken off so that I could

be grafted in." Granted. But they were broken off because
of unbelief, and you stand by faith. Do not be arrogant,
but be afraid. For if God did not spare the natural branches,
he will not spare you either.
Consider therefore the kindness and sternness of God:
sternness to those who fell, but kindness to you, provided that
you continue in his kindness. Otherwise, you also will be cut
off. And if they do not persist in unbelief, they will be grafted
in, for God is able to graft them in again. After all, if you
were cut out of an olive tree that is wild by nature, and
contrary to nature were grafted into a cultivated olive tree,
how much more readily will these, the natural branches, be
grafted into their own olive tree!
I do not want you to be ignorant of this mystery, brothers,
so that you may not be conceited: Israel has experienced a
hardening in part until the full number of the Gentiles has
come in. And so all Israel will be saved, as it is written:
"The deliverer will come from Zion; he will turn Godlessness
away from Jacob. And this is my covenant with them when
I take away their sins."

A RICH HERITAGE OF FAITH

With that in mind, remember that almost all of the early Church were Jewish converts. By age six, many Jewish children had memorized most, if not all, of the Torah (the first five books of Moses). They had a rich, deep heritage based on God's law. When the Gospel spread, the later converts were pagans who had been taught Greek philosophy. Those new believers began blending Christianity with their pagan beliefs.

One man, Origin, is considered to be the most influential theologian of the early Church. He took principles of Neo-Platonism, which included elements of mysticism and some Judaic and Christian concepts, and blended them into theology. He also blended stoicism, an ancient Greek religion that equates God with the totality of the universe. He created a system to interpret the Bible using allegory and spiritualization. He was the originator of the concept that God had rejected the Jews and replaced them with the Church.

Another man who did immeasurable damage to the Gospel was Augustine, who is considered the founder of theology. According to *Columbia Encyclopedia*, Augustine incorporated Plato's doctrines and Neo-Platonism into Christian theology. As a consequence, salvation was redefined. The Bible said, "We believe *in* Jesus." The Greek mindset said, "We believe *that...*" Changing one word caused people to believe heaven was reserved for the doctrinally correct, which splintered the Church into different groups supporting different theologies of salvation. This sparked more than 1,700 years of doctrinal war within the Church, draining it of power.

> Another man who did immeasurable damage to the Gospel was Augustine.

Prior to this, the Church had been the recipient of thousands of years of Jewish history. Sometime around the sixth century the Messianic Church died, and we dropped our Jewish roots. In other words, we cut off the branch we're grafted into! When this happened, the Church as a whole lost the power and the signs, wonders, and miracles that the early Church enjoyed.

There are churches, such as Bethel Church in Redding, California, pastored by Bill Johnson, that operate with signs and wonders. I believe this is in part because they have re-grafted themselves into the tree of their Jewish roots. Of course, there are others, but the miraculous has become the minority and the exception rather than the rule in the Church today. I believe that very soon there will be a tipping point where the Church as a whole will re-graft ourselves back into the olive tree, and then the power will flow as it did in the times of Pentecost.

ONE NEW MAN

Our Lord is a God of restoration, and in the sixteenth century, He restored the doctrine of salvation. In the eighteenth century, there was a restoration of holiness. In the twentieth century, there was the restoration of gifts. But we as a Church have not re-grafted ourselves back into the tree. The sap hasn't run into our branch in at least 1,400 years, so we have no power. We must repent for trying to make ourselves the root when God said we were a branch grafted into the olive tree, which was Israel.

In reality, Origin and Augustine were the worst enemies of the Church. Because of their teaching, we divorced our Jewish heritage and married paganism. Now we must divorce paganism and remarry our Jewish roots. When we do that, the scales will fall off of the eyes of the Jews, and the Messianic Church will explode in growth. The Gentiles and the Jews together will become the One New Man that Paul described in Ephesians 2:11–17: "Therefore, remember that formerly you who are Gentiles by birth and called 'uncircumcised' by those who call themselves 'the circumcision' (that done in the body by the hands of men)—remember that at that time you were separate from Christ, excluded from citizenship in Israel and foreigners to the covenants of the promise, without hope and without God in the world. But now in Christ Jesus you who once were far away have been brought near through the blood of Christ. For he himself is our peace, who has made the two one and has destroyed the barrier, the dividing wall of hostility, by abolishing in his flesh the law with its commandments and regulations. His purpose was to create in himself *one new man* out of the two, thus making peace, and in this one body to reconcile both of them to God through the cross, by which he put to death their hostility." (emphasis mine)

> Our Lord is a God of restoration

129

OPPOSING GOD

One key strategy for winning every battle is to look deep into your heart and repent if there is any anti-Semitism there. Why? When you oppose Israel, even in your heart, you are opposing Israel's covenant partner—God. The truth is that you won't win any battles if you find yourself opposing God. You will win every battle if God is fighting on your behalf.

There's something else dangerous about anti-Semitism. The Bible says that one day Jesus will return just as He left. People get excited about that without stopping to consider who Jesus was on earth. He was a Jewish rabbi. That means He will return as a Jewish rabbi.

"Wait a minute, Mike," you might say, "look what happened to the Jews during the Holocaust. It looks to me like God abandoned them."

God will never abandon the Jewish people, because of His covenant with Abraham. However, when they rebelled against God and worshipped idols, they stepped outside of God's protection, and the devil tried to kill them. In spite of their sin, God not only saved them, He kept His promise to give them back their land and restore Israel as a nation.

That's how faithful God is to His chosen people. In addition to the personal judgment we each face after death, the Bible says that God will judge each nation on earth. How will He judge them? They will be judged by how they treated Israel. Part of the reason the United States has been so blessed by God is because, historically, we have been a friend and ally to Israel.

None of this makes sense until you begin to grasp the concept of covenant.

GOD'S ORDER

Let's say that I have a friend named Larry who is dying. Larry has been a good friend to me over the years, and I want to bless him. I visit him and say, "Larry, you've been a good friend and a blessing in my life, so now I want to be a blessing to you. You have a wife and five children; I have wealth and power. I give you my word that I will take care of your wife and children for the rest of their lives. In the event of my death, I'm leaving a trust for them along with very specific instructions regarding their care. I promise you that your family will lack for nothing."

> God will never abandon the Jews because of His covenant with Abraham.

In its simplest form, that's what God did for the Jews. He plucked Abraham out of obscurity, became his friend, made a covenant with him and promised to take care of his descendents throughout all the generations to come. So long as there is a descendent of Abraham, Isaac, and Jacob alive on earth, God will watch over him and defend him.

"Wait a minute!" someone argued. "There's got to be a time limit on this covenant God made!

This subject is clarified in the Bible numerous times, but here is just one scripture that addresses it.

> *He remembers his covenant forever,*
> *the word he commanded,*
> *for a thousand generations,*
> *the covenant he made with Abraham,*
> *the oath he swore to Isaac.*
> *He confirmed it to Jacob as a decree,*
> *to Israel as an everlasting covenant:*
> *"To you I will give the land of Canaan*
> *as the portion you will inherit."*
> PSALM 105:8–11

Christianity can trace its roots all the way back to Abraham. Everything started with the Jews; they are God's First People. If you oppose them, you oppose God. If you bless them, God will bless you. All you have to do is look at the universe to know that God has an order to everything. God's order is the Jews first and Gentiles (everyone else) second. When you try to relate to God apart from His covenant with Abraham, you're swimming upstream, and you won't prosper.

PRAY FOR JERUSALEM

This concept is true in our personal lives, it's true in business, and it's true for nations. If you want to be successful, pray for and bless the Jews. One of the admonitions in the Bible is that we should pray for the peace of Jerusalem. Psalm 122:6–9 says: "Pray for the peace of Jerusalem: 'May those who love you be secure. May there be peace within your walls and security within your citadels.' For the sake of my brothers and friends, I will say, 'Peace be within you.' For the sake of the house of the LORD our God, I will seek your prosperity."

> God will judge each nation on earth by how they treated Israel.

This is a prayer that should forever be on our hearts and our lips. It's also a prayer that should be in our arsenal of weapons. There have been times in my life when it seemed as though a dark cloud followed me around that I couldn't shake. When that happened, I prayed this prayer for Jerusalem. It releases such power that clouds of doom dissipate—they have to flee.

We've all seen a doting father who melts when we do something nice for his child. We inherited that characteristic from God. When you bless Israel, He will melt before your eyes and bless you beyond your wildest dreams.

THE BLESSING OF THE LORD

"Wait a minute!" someone said. "The Jews have been persecuted beyond belief. The nation of Israel has been under attack almost since its inception. It doesn't sound to me like God has blessed them."

That's a very good point. What constitutes the blessing of God? The Bible gives the answer in Proverbs 10:22, "The blessing of the

LORD makes one rich, and He adds no sorrow with it." The word *blessing* in that verse means "prosperity, a gift, a present and a treaty of peace." With that definition in mind, is there any evidence that God's blessing still rests on the Jewish people?

In a world brimming with six billion people, only 13 million are Jews. They represent one-fifth of one percent of the world population, a tiny minority. In addition to their dwindling population, consider their tenuous position in the Middle East:

"Since independence in May 1948, Israel has fought six wars, two intifadas, a continuing terrorism threat, an economic boycott, and intermittent diplomatic isolation. It is currently in a formal state of war with two of its neighbors (Syria and Lebanon) and has only a cool peace with the other two (Jordan and Egypt), despite peace treaties. In effect, all of its land borders are relatively closed to trade. More generally, it is an outcast in the Middle East, deprived of any opportunity to benefit from the commerce generated by regional oil wealth but having to bear the costs of living in a neighborhood characterized by arms races and instability."[2]

> Israel's economy is larger than the combination of all its near neighbors.

Israel is no more than a tiny strip of land situated in a hotbed of hatred in the Middle East. It is the 100th smallest nation, boasting only 1/1000th of the world's population. Yet, Israel's economy is larger than the combination of all its near neighbors. It is the only liberal democracy in the Middle East and has the highest average standard of living in the Middle East. Except for the United States, it has more start-up companies than any country on earth. On a per capita basis, Israel has the largest number of biotech start ups. It is ranked second in the world for venture capital funds. Israel has the highest number of NASDAQ companies outside of the U.S. and Canada. It leads the world in the number of scientists and technicians.

With the exception of Silicon Valley, Israel has the highest concentration of high-tech companies in the world. The cell phone, voicemail, most of the Windows NT operating system, the Pentium MMX Chip technology, the technology for AOL instant messaging, and the first PC antivirus software were all developed in Israel.[3]

It is impossible to deny that the blessing of the Lord rests on Israel. What about Jews who live elsewhere? In the United States, for example, Jews make up only two percent of the population, and many Jewish-Americans have only been in this country for one or two generations. In his book, *The Phenomenon of the Jews: Seven Keys to the Enduring Wealth of a People,* author Steven Silbiger makes the following observation:

"Steven Spielberg. Ralph Lauren. Michael Eisner. Michael Dell. They're all successful, at the top of their fields. They're all fabulously wealthy. And they're all Jewish. Those three characteristics—successful, wealthy, and Jewish—are linked repeatedly in America today. And it is no accident. Jewish Americans are, as a group, the wealthiest ethnic group in America."

> Whole books have been written in an effort to determine how this tiny minority of people, who have been persecuted almost to the point of extinction, could amass such wealth.

Silbiger goes on to point out that the percentage of Jewish households with an income greater than $50,000 is double that of non-Jews. They make up 45 percent of the top 40 of the richest Americans listed by Forbes 400. One third of all American multimillionaires are Jewish. Thirty percent of American Nobel prize winners in science and 25 percent of all American Nobel winners are Jewish.

Whole books, including the one just mentioned, have been written in an effort to determine how this tiny minority of people, who have been persecuted almost to the point of extinction, could amass such wealth. None of the theories factor in their covenant with God. Nor do they consider this simple truth: The blessing of the Lord makes one rich.

SORROW ADDED

If you've followed the lives of people who won huge sums of money in the lottery, you know that most of them didn't have the wisdom or the strength of character to pass the test of prosperity. They became rich, but great sorrow was added to it. Most of them lost the money and ended up in worse shape than they were in before they won it.

Why does that happen? Is it because God doesn't want us rich? Is it because poverty makes us humble? *No.* In 3 John 2, God's will is made clear. "Beloved, I pray that in all respects you may prosper and be in good health, just as your soul prospers" (NASB).

Notice that God equates prosperity with how your soul is doing. Your soul is made up of your mind, will, and emotions. The problem with some of the lottery winners was that their soul—their mind, will, and emotions—hadn't prospered and matured in the Lord. They didn't have the wisdom needed to handle that much money.

Don't be mistaken, if you're in covenant with God, His plan is to make you rich. However, in the process He will cause your soul to prosper. Our souls prosper when our minds are renewed to God's Word—the Bible. Our souls prosper when we spend time worshiping God and journaling.

> *Beloved, I pray that in all respects you may prosper and be in good health, just as your soul prospers.*
> 3 JOHN 2 (NASB)

Part of the misconception about money is the belief that money is the root of all evil. That's not true; the Bible doesn't say that. The Bible says that the *love* of money is the root of all kinds of evil.

The way you can enjoy prosperity and have no sorrow added to it is by *loving God* and using money. That's why one way that we ratify our covenant with God is through giving our tithes and offerings. A tithe is one tenth of all our income. Offerings include anything you give over and above the tithe. It's a lot easier for some people to trust God with their souls for eternity than to trust Him with their finances. The root of that fear is the love of money.

Every time you give your tithe and offering, you are cutting off the love of money. You may begin as a child by tithing ten cents on your dollar allowance. Over time, as you prove yourself faithful in the small amounts, God will bless you with more. Each time you are faithful and obedient to give God His portion first, your soul prospers. When God makes you rich, you won't have any trouble writing a tithe check for more than your annual salary used to be. In fact, you'll do it with joy.

DEALING WITH THE DEVIL

The Bible says that when you give God the first tenth of your income that He will deal with the devil, whose goal is to steal your money. So each time you give your tithe, or an offering over and above the tithe, you are not only ratifying your covenant with God, you're involving God in your finances. He'll bless your money like He did the fish and loaves of bread until there are basketsful left over. When God blesses you and makes you rich, there is no sorrow added.

> He'll bless your money like He did the fish and loaves of bread until there are basketsful left over.

God will bless your personal finances, and He'll bless your business. He'll do the same thing for you that He has done for Israel. He'll give you unusual wisdom, creative ideas, and witty inventions. He'll bless your brain and cause you to be more intelligent than your competitors. He'll show you the strategy to win every battle. When everything is on the line, if you ask, He'll whisper the answer you need in your ear. If you don't listen, He'll shout until you hear Him.

"Mike," you might say, "I'm a Christian, and I'm in covenant with God, but my business is hemorrhaging money."

In chapter four I explained that there is a very real spirit called fear. There are also spirits of poverty, lack, and debt who will try to steal your blessing. There is no poverty, lack, or debt in God's kingdom, so anytime those three hoodlums linger around your home or business, use the name of Jesus to chase them back to hell where they belong. You must say aloud, "I take authority over you spirit of fear. In the mighty name of Jesus and through His blood, I bind you and send you away never to return." The words "take authority" are very important. Those thugs are the counterfeit. Command them to leave and then invite the Holy Spirit to bring the spirit of prosperity to bless your finances and your business. Those evil spirits must leave. Remember, I'm not a preacher. I'm a businessman and—bottom line—this works.

Sometimes the Lord will have you give an offering that will remove the noose that's strangling your finances. As strange as it may sound, I love to give into the kingdom of God. My primary motivation is love. I love God so much that I want to be a blessing to Him. I've also learned that you just can't out give God. No matter how much you give, He finds a way to open the windows of heaven and pour out even greater bountiful blessings over you. I also enjoy giving to God because I know that it gets Him even more involved with my finances. I want Him involved in every detail of my life.

THE MULTIPLICATION FACTOR

Years ago when I first heard a pastor explain the concept of tithing, I wanted to weep, because I realized I'd been robbing God. I started writing tithe checks, and it was glorious. Not long ago I learned about the Jewish custom of giving a First Fruits offering. For instance, during biblical days someone might chose to give a First Fruits offering, thanking God in advance for a harvest. Likewise, today we can give First Fruits offerings in anticipation of some blessing from God.

I'd never heard about a First Fruits offering in my life, but there it was in black and white print in my Bible (Exodus 23; 34; Leviticus 2; 23). I wanted to lie down and weep, because I'd never known about it. I knew that God was going to hit some of my business deals out of the ballpark, but I didn't want to wait until then to thank Him. I wanted God to know that I trusted Him and thanked Him *now* before I ever saw a nickel of the money.

I wanted God to know that the offering was meaningful to me, so I wrote a check large enough that it hurt. I took the check to my church and offered it to God. I told my pastor, "I've never given God a First Fruits offering because I didn't know about them. I want you to know that I am thanking God in advance for what He will do on my behalf. I'll be back in the near future and tell you a story of what God did for me that will blow your mind."

I've noticed a strange paradox; everyone wants and needs money, but they get nervous when you talk about giving. Don't think I'm leading up to something, because I don't need or want your money. Your money and what you do with it are between you and God, but never forget that giving is an act of covenant. You might have a dozen strikes against you in the battle that you're fighting. You might believe you're the wrong color, the wrong gender, or the wrong age, but when you're in covenant with God, none of that matters. God will do for you what He did for his First People, the Jews.

He will bless you above all the people on the earth.

When I asked for an A in one of my toughest classes, God looked at me and saw His covenant with me through His Son, Jesus. That would never have happened had I not walked through that Door, who is Jesus, and become One with Him.

What does that mean in practical terms? It means that when you surrender your life to Jesus, all the blessings of Abraham are yours...and more. It means that if you're a first-year law student about to crash and burn, and you ask God for help, He will whisper the answer you need to know in your ear. God loves revealing mysteries to His people.

LOOKING AT REVELATION BACKWARD

I believe that those of us privileged enough to live on earth during this particular time are blessed and highly favored by God. Among other things, one of those blessings is that we are alive when the revelation in the book of Daniel has been unsealed by God. In other words, out of all the believers in the history of the world, we were chosen to receive the mystery that has been sealed inside the book of Daniel for thousands of years.

In the twelfth chapter, Daniel records receiving a puzzling vision that he didn't understand.

> *I heard, but I did not understand. So I asked, "My Lord, what will the outcome of all this be?"*
> *He replied, "Go your way, Daniel, because the words are closed up and sealed until the time of the end. Many will be purified, made spotless and refined, but the wicked will continue to be wicked. None of the wicked will understand, but those who are wise will understand. From the time that the daily sacrifice is abolished and the abomination that causes desolation is set up, there will be 1,290 days."*
> DANIEL 12:8–11

This scripture passage has puzzled people for many years and left them asking the following questions. What is the message hidden in Daniel, and when will it be revealed? What is the abomination of desolation, and when will it happen? What is the significance of 1,290 days?

God has unsealed many of the answers to these questions. Without a doubt, the days mentioned by Daniel were not days as we know them. In 2 Peter 3:8, we read, "But do not forget this one thing, dear friends: With the Lord a day is like a thousand years, and a thousand years are like a day." By this we know that God's days and our days are very different.

In order to calculate the events mentioned in Daniel, we must take into account that the Old Testament was written in Hebrew and based on the Hebrew calendar. The New Testament was written in Greek and is based on the solar calendar. The conversion factor to change the Hebrew year into the solar year is .9857.

THE ABOMINATION THAT CAUSES DESOLATION

One of the great mysteries of the book of Daniel has been the abomination of desolation. Most of us have been taught that this refers to a man—the anti-Christ. However, if you ask any Jew about the abomination of desolation, they will tell you that it happened when the Muslims built the Dome of the Rock on the temple mount.

Is it possible that we've missed the obvious all these years? In order to test that theory, we must look again at Daniel 12:11: "From the time that the daily sacrifice is abolished and the abomination that causes desolation is set up, there will be 1,290 days."

We know that the sacrifices stopped around 583 B.C. From that point until the abomination of desolation is 1,290 days. In order to convert from the Hebrew calendar, we multiply 1290 x .9857 (the conversion factor) = 1271.55.

1271.55 is the exact number of years from when the sacrifices stopped in 583 B.C. until the Dome of the Rock began construction on the temple mount in A.D. 688! Therefore, without question, the abomination that causes desolation occurred in A.D. 688 when the Muslims began building the Dome of the Rock.

SACRIFICES STOPPED   DOME OF THE ROCK

1271.55

583 B.C.   A.D. 688

MEASURING THE TEMPLE

One of the problems we've had in understanding the end times, and particularly the book of Revelation, has been that we read it looking forward to the future. Since the desolation that causes abomination has already occurred, now we can read some of these events looking back in time.

For instance, Revelation 11:1–2 says, "I was given a reed like a measuring rod and was told, 'Go and measure the temple of God and the altar, and count the worshipers there. But exclude the outer court; do not measure it, because it has been given to the Gentiles. They will trample on the holy city for 42 months.'"

Using our conversion table, a solar year is 365.24 days. Divide those days by the 12 months in a year and you'll have a monthly average of 30.44 days. Multiply 30.44 days by 42 months and you'll get 1278.34 years (or days of years). If you add 1278.34 years to 688.66, when the Dome of the Rock had begun to be built on the temple mount, the answer will be 1967. That was a very significant year in the history of Israel. During June 5–10, 1967, Israel fought against Egypt, Jordan, and Syria in what was known as the Six Day War. Iraq, Saudi Arabia, Sudan, Tunisia, Morocco, and Algeria also contributed troops and arms to the Arab armies. Vastly outnumbered, Israel captured the Gaza Strip and the Sinai Peninsula from Egypt, the West Bank—including East Jerusalem—from Jordan, and the Golan Heights from Syria. 1967 marked the year Jerusalem was freed just as Revelation 11:1–2 said it would happen.

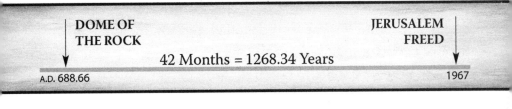

DOME OF
THE ROCK

JERUSALEM
FREED

42 Months = 1268.34 Years

A.D. 688.66

1967

BUILT ON THE WRONG ROCK

On the temple site in Jerusalem, there were two flat rocks. One of them marked the site of the Holy of Holies. The other was located 300 feet south of the Holy of Holies. When the temple was still in use, anyone could go into the outer court, even a pagan. However, only those priests who had cleansed themselves from sin and been sanctified and set apart to God could enter the Holy of Holies. That's the site the Muslims wanted to desecrate when they built the Dome of the Rock. Part of their heritage is that they always want to worship from the highest, most sacred point. Therefore they assumed that the flat rock on the south end of the temple would have been the location for the Holy of Holies.

They built on the wrong Rock—both literally and figuratively! Their greatest miscalculation was to build their spiritual heritage on Muhammed instead of Jesus. Their second miscalculation was that they miscalculated the location of the Holy of Holies. Choosing the wrong Rock, they built the Dome of the Rock 300 feet south of the site of the Holy of Holies. They built in the Outer Court!

Looking again at Revelation 11:1–2 (NKJV), it's no wonder that God told the angel not to measure the outer court. "Then I was given a reed like a measuring rod. And the angel stood, saying, 'Rise and measure the temple of God, the altar, and those who worship there. But leave out the court which is outside the temple, and do not measure it, for it has been given to the Gentiles. And they will tread the holy city underfoot for forty-two months.'"

I want to add one note here regarding the Arab nations. Modern-day Arabs claim descent from Ishmael, the son of Abraham and Sarah's Egyptian maidservant, Hagar (Genesis 16; 25). The thousands of years of enmity between the sons of Ishmael and the sons of Isaac have caused the Abrahamic family to remain incomplete. There is a seat at the family table that will never be filled until the sons of Ishmael take their place there. God desires those sons to return home and take their seat of honor.

SEVENTY WEEKS AND THE MESSIAH

Another fascinating scripture passage is found in the Daniel 9.

> *"Seventy weeks have been decreed for your people and your holy city, to finish the transgression, to make an end of sin, to make atonement for iniquity, to bring in everlasting righteousness, to seal up vision and prophecy and to anoint the most holy place.*
> *"So you are to know and discern that from the issuing of a decree to restore and rebuild Jerusalem until Messiah the Prince there will be seven weeks and sixty-two weeks; it will be built again, with plaza and moat, even in times of distress. Then after the sixty-two weeks the Messiah will be cut off and have nothing, and the people of the prince who is to come will destroy the city and the sanctuary."*
> DANIEL 9:24–26 NASB

Daniel prophesied that there would be a period of 7 weeks and 62 weeks from the decree to restore and rebuild Jerusalem until the following things happen:

1. To finish transgression.
2. To make an end of sin.
3. To make an atonement for iniquity.
4. To bring in everlasting righteousness.

Then, after 62 weeks, the Messiah will be cut off and have nothing. The timeline looks like this:

FROM THE DECREE OF ARTAXERXES I TO REBUILD THE WALLS	OLD TESTAMENT CANON CLOSES	CRUCIFIXION MESSIAH "CUT OFF"
7 weeks = 48.3 years	62 weeks = 427.7 years	
444-445 B.C.	396 B.C.	A.D. 32-33

476 YEARS

God's calculations never miss the mark. From the decree of Artaxerxes I to rebuild the walls of Jerusalem until the crucifixion was the exact period prophesied by Daniel. When the Messiah was "cut off" by crucifixion, Jesus' blood sacrifice accomplished everything mentioned in Daniel 9. Among other things, on the cross Jesus finished transgression, made an end of sin, made atonement for iniquity, and brought about everlasting righteousness.

Why am I telling you this? I mentioned earlier that God doesn't micromanage what happens on earth. We have been given authority over this earth, and we have an enemy who has brought sin, sickness, evil, and heartache to the world. However, God does macromanage all of His major plot points in history. As you have seen through these examples, right down to the smallest millisecond, He has ordered certain events. On a worldwide scale, there is no devil or demon powerful enough to stop the plan of God from being fulfilled. If you will learn to live in covenant and in intimacy with God, there is no devil or demon powerful enough to stop His supernatural intervention in your life.

No plot or plan of the enemy can stop you from winning every battle.

BATTLE PLAN

Covenant is the process of becoming As One with God. It's impossible to win every battle unless you're in covenant with Him. And it's impossible to win every battle if you oppose God by opposing His chosen people. However, if you are in covenant with God, not only will you win every battle, God will also bless you above all the nations on the earth.

BATTLE PRINCIPLES:

- You have to participate in the New Covenant through Jesus' shed blood in order to be As One with God.

- Proverbs 10:22 promises that, "The blessing of the LORD makes one rich, and He adds no sorrow with it."

- The Bible makes it clear that part of God's blessing involves prosperity. In 3 John 2, we read, "Beloved, I pray that in all respects you may prosper and be in good health, just as your soul prospers."

- The Bible says that when you give God the first tenth of your income that He will deal with the devil, whose goal is to steal your money.

- Every time you give your tithe and offering, you are cutting off the love of money.

- Whenever you involve God in your finances, He will bless them like He blessed the fish and loaves of bread; He will multiply them until there are basketfuls left over.

BATTLE STRATEGIES:

THE FIRST STEP: Settle Covenant Issues
If you didn't get this settled in chapter one, get your covenant with God settled forever by repenting of your sins and giving your life to Jesus. Meet with your pastor or a trusted spiritual leader if you have questions.

THE SECOND STEP: Educate Yourself
Do a word search and study the covenants listed in the Bible. Read books or listen to teachings regarding the benefits of covenant with God.

THE THIRD STEP: Get Rid of Anti-Semitism
If there is even a hint of anti-Semitism in your heart, repent and get rid of it. If you oppose God's chosen people, He will oppose you.

THE FOURTH STEP: Pray for the Peace of Jerusalem
Make it a daily habit to pray for the peace of Jerusalem. "'May those who love you be secure. May there be peace within your walls and security within your citadels.' For the sake of my brothers and friends, I will say, 'Peace be within you.' For

the sake of the house of the Lord our God, I will seek your prosperity" (Psalm 122:6–9).

THE FIFTH STEP: *Give Tithes as an Act of Covenant*
Giving the first tenth of all your income is an act of covenant and the best way to protect your finances.

THE SIXTH STEP: *Remove the Noose*
Sometimes the Lord will have you give an offering that will remove the noose that's strangling your finances. Ask God for His strategy. A First Fruits offering is given in anticipation of a blessing from God.

THE SEVENTH STEP: *Ask!*
When you're in covenant with God, repent of any known sin and ask Him for what you need. He'll whisper the answer into your ear. If you aren't listening, He may shout.

FINDING
YOUR DESTINY

D*obie!* I bolted out of bed and ran downstairs certain that Dobie would launch himself into my arms and lick the sleep out of my eyes. There was no answering bark of joy; no passionate package of unconditional love to greet me. I sank onto the back step and looked across the lawn where Dobie should have been sunning himself. At 14, I was too old to cry, but I couldn't swallow the lump in my throat and my eyes burned with unshed tears. Dobie had wandered away before, but his adventures sniffing out the neighbors' bushes had been brief. He always came home.

I stared at his food and water bowls. They hadn't been touched since the day before. Wherever he was, Dobie had to be hungry and thirsty. Was he hurt? I choked back a sob. Was he dead? The whole family was sad, mourning the loss of the friendliest and happiest one among us.

"He must have gotten lost," my mother said, sorrow dimming her eyes.

"He may have been hit by a car," my dad said, shaking his head.

Dobie wasn't a prize dog, nor was he a purebred. He was some kind of hybrid Dachshund with short legs that peddled as he slept, dreaming, I was certain, of running to me. He's sort of goofy looking, I admitted. The thing about Dobie was that...he was *ours*.

I stood up, a determined glint in my eye. Dobie was ours, and I was going to find him. Running upstairs, I dressed before mapping out my strategy. I divided our neighborhood and the surrounding area into a grid pattern. If I searched each section of the grid in a methodical and systematic manner, in time I would have searched the entire area.

THE SEARCH

I raced to the garage and kick started my 50cc Honda Mini Trail. Starting at one corner of my grid, I slowed the bike to a crawl and searched front yards, back yards, and alleys. I made myself hoarse yelling, "DOBIE!" I asked everyone I saw if they'd seen him; no one had.

> He's sort of goofy looking, I admitted, wiping my nose on the sleeve of my pajamas. The thing about Dobie was that...he was *ours*.

Just stick to your plan, I told myself hours later when I stopped to fill the Honda's tank with gas. Wiping sweat from my eyes, I picked up where I'd left off. At dusk, tired, hungry, and discouraged, I went home for dinner.

Dobie! The next morning I raced downstairs hoping against hope that Dobie would greet me. He hadn't come home. I grabbed some fruit, dressed, and started my minibike. Picking up where I'd left off the evening before, I started searching each section of the grid. "DOBIE!" I shouted loud enough that he could hear me over the minibike.

"I can do this," I told myself over and over when I was tempted to go hang out with my friends rather than stick to the mind-numbing search. With each passing hour, my heart felt heavier. If Dobie were alive, how long would he have gone without food and water? I *had* to find him.

I lost count of the number of times I stopped to refill my gas tank. At dusk, as the sun dipped below the horizon, I dragged myself home. Where *was* he? What had happened to him? I couldn't imagine how scared he must be.

I tossed and turned in bed that night, fighting off nightmares of what I would see when I found Dobie. The next morning, I ran across the kitchen knowing before I ever opened the door that Dobie wasn't there. I looked at the blazing sun and knew that if Dobie was alive, there was no time to waste. I drove to the spot where I'd stopped the night before and started my search again.

"DOBIE!"

> I looked at the blazing sun and knew that if Dobie was alive, there was no time to waste.

HOPELESS

By afternoon, I'd left the neighborhood and was searching 160 acres of open fields. Grief rose up from deep within me. I had been sure that I could find Dobie. My search pattern...my grid...my plan seemed fail proof. I'd done everything I knew to do, but it wasn't enough.

Dobie needed a miracle. In that moment of total despair, I surrendered to God. From the depths of my being, I screamed. "GOD, HELP ME FIND MY DOG!"

I was alone in the field. Yet seconds later, I heard an audible voice, loud and commanding.

"STOP!" The word echoed through every molecule of my being.

Chills raced up my spine as I let off the gas and braked to a stop. Over the soft purr of the idling engine, I heard what sounded like a whimper. I threw my minibike aside and ran toward the sound. Forty feet to my side was a giant bush, like a tree that had grown into a hedge. It was at least 12 feet tall and just as wide.

"DOBIE!" I screamed.

I heard a weak yelp. Throwing myself into the hedge, I fought branches that clawed and slapped me. At the center of the bush, his leash wrapped around the trunk, sat Dobie. I could have sworn that his eyes misted when he saw me, a look that said, *I knew you'd come.* I untangled his leash, and Dobie leapt into my arms.

> Without God's intervention, I would have driven right past him, never knowing what happened to him.

At home, Dobie's belly full of food and water, he fell asleep in my arms. He dreamed, making soft barking noises, his legs peddling as he ran. My mind circled around the Voice that had commanded me to stop.

I'd screamed to God for help, and He'd answered me. Without that command to stop, I would never have heard Dobie's cries over the noise of the engine. Without God's intervention, I would have driven right past him, never knowing what happened to him.

I fell asleep with an ache as deep as the urge to find Dobie had been. My last conscious thought was of the God who found my dog. I wanted to find God. I wanted to know Him. I didn't want to live my life without Him.

THE SEARCH FOR DESTINY

That encounter with God when I was 14 years old left a hunger in me for Him. That's why, when I was 16 and someone told me how I could invite God into my life, I leapt at the chance. Who *wouldn't* want that kind of supernatural power available in their lives?

I know that those moments were divine encounters that moved me toward my destiny. As I look around the world today, it seems to me that when it comes to finding their destiny, a lot of people are as lost as Dobie was. As they wandered through life, like Dobie, they got stuck somewhere, and that's where they stayed. Like him, a lot of people don't know how to get unstuck and move on to their destiny.

God may have called you to play the piano and change the music industry. If you're a writer, God will use you to change that industry. I'm in the real estate development business, and God will affect that industry through me. For years, everywhere I worked I made money for other people. It wasn't until I was 48 years old that God released me to start my own business. When that happened, my income didn't just increase, it multiplied exponentially.

Wealth isn't just about money; it's about joy, happiness, peace, and favor with both God and men. It's about God opening the right doors and our stepping through them at the right time. It's about fulfilling our destiny. However, when you're in covenant with God, His blessing will make you rich. Although God caused me to prosper all the years that I worked for other people, until I learned to walk out the principles in this book on a daily basis, I wasn't in a position to receive wealth. My soul hadn't prospered enough to handle it.

> As I look around the world today, it seems to me that when it comes to finding their destiny, a lot of people are as lost as Dobie was.

Don't misunderstand, God blessed me and provided for me well. But until I got the principles in this book down in my heart and working in my life, I wasn't ready to handle the wealth. God loved me too much to put me in a situation where I could fail. Defeat and failure are not in His vocabulary. God has a mindset of victory; He has never lost a battle, and He never will.

As soon as I learned to use these principles to win every battle, God opened the windows of heaven and poured out His blessings over me. He'll do the same thing for you. The difference is that what took me years to learn, you can learn in a matter of months, weeks, or days. It's possible to get yourself or your business in position for a miracle in a day. It could be done in a day by General Motors. It could be done in a day by Chrysler, Ford, or Xerox. There's no situation too desperate for God to repair.

A GLIMPSE OF YOURSELF

God is always willing to do His part. What takes the longest is for us to use the Bible like a mirror and discover who we are in Christ. You would be so shocked if you could glimpse yourself through God's eyes. One way you can do that is to read what God says about you in the Bible.

For instance, a lot of people think of themselves as worms in God's sight. That's not what God says! According to the Bible, we are kings and priests!

"To Him who loved us and washed us from our sins in His own blood, and has made us kings and priests to His God and Father" (Revelation 1:6 NKJV).

"Wait a minute, Mike!" you might say. "I'm not a king or a priest!"

If you're going to win every battle, it's a good idea to agree with God, and God says you are. Part of the confusion lies in the fact that you may not be a priest in the usual sense of the word. For instance, you may never be in the employ of a church, wear the mantle of a priest, and offer sacraments. But that doesn't mean you're not a priest. When you wake each morning and worship the Lord, giving Him the sacrifice of praise and offering to Him the sacrament of your life...you are a priest unto God. You are worshipping at His altar, whether it is the altar at a church or the altar of your heart.

> If you're going to win every battle, it's a good idea to agree with God

Likewise, the reason that the idea of being a king is confusing is because here in America, we don't understand the culture of a kingdom. When Jesus walked the earth doing miracles and teaching people who they were called to be, He said on numerous occasions, "The kingdom of God has come to you." As one of God's children, you have the rights and privileges of His royal family. In short, you are a king who is helping to run the family business.

THE KING'S DOMAIN

A kingdom is the king's domain, and God's kingdom cannot be limited to the brick and mortar walls of a church building. God's kingdom is all the earth, which includes the marketplace. You may be surprised to know that the vast majority of the miracles recorded in the New Testament occurred, not in the temple, but in the marketplace. God has kings in banking, in construction, in agriculture, in government, in education, and in every arena of life. If you haven't been called to work in a church, you are called to work wherever God has planted you. For most of us, that means we are called, anointed, and appointed as kings and priests in the marketplace.

For too long we believed that those called to work in the Church were whom God had called to do the work of the ministry. That's *not* what the Bible says. God called and gifted apostles, prophets, evangelists, pastors, and teachers in the Church so that they could equip *us* to do the work of the ministry in the marketplace. This is explained in Ephesians 4:11–12: "And He Himself gave some to be apostles, some prophets, some evangelists, and some pastors and teachers, *for the equipping of the saints for the work of ministry*" (NKJV, emphasis mine).

FINDING OUR NEW IDENTITY

I know it may be a shock to your system, but not only does God call us kings and priests, He calls us saints. Not all of us are called to be apostles, prophets, evangelists, pastors, or teachers, but all of us are called to be saints who carry out the work of the ministry right where we are. The greatest shift in our paradigm may be learning to change our perception of ourselves. Most of us don't know that we have miracles in our mouth. We don't know that the quickest route to victory is total surrender. We don't know that unforgiveness, bitterness, or judgment will stop God's blessings cold. We don't even know all that God offered to us in our covenant.

In other words, we don't fulfill our destiny because we don't know His plan for our lives. Each of us has a two-part destiny. I can tell you the first and most important thing God has called you to do with your life. Are you ready?

> The greatest thing you have been created and destined to do is to have an intimate relationship with God. That is the highest call in your life.

The greatest thing you have been created and destined to do is to have an intimate relationship with God. That is the highest call in your life.

How do you discover the second part of your destiny? You ask. You could do like I did when I screamed, "God, help me find my dog!" But you don't have to scream, because you have an intimate relationship with Him. First, you worship your way into His presence. Then you ask. God will answer. If you don't hear the answer right away, don't be discouraged. Keep listening. Keep seeking. Keep searching for God's heart. He will reveal it to you.

GOD'S MANTLE

If you've ever watched a coronation service on television, you know that in addition to the crown, the king or queen wears a robe that signifies their authority. Strange as it may seem, as a king and priest before God, you have been given a mantle of leadership. Have you ever wondered why, when life keeps knocking you down, you always float back up to the top? It's because God's mantle rests upon you.

Let's say that you were called to the marketplace as a chef. You loved to cook and prepare beautiful meals, but your first job was behind the bar of a greasy diner. Over time, you worked your way up to the position of head chef in a fabulous French restaurant. Some days, you looked around and wondered how that happened. However, demographics changed and business declined. In time, the restaurant closed. While hundreds of other chefs were out of work,

God made a way for you to open your own restaurant. He made you a king in the world of restaurants.

Things like that happen every day in the lives of people in covenant with God. It happens because God has given them a destiny and a mantle for success.

God is searching the world to find men and women who will accept their mantle as kings in the marketplace. I encourage you to have a coronation ceremony in your own mind. Tell the Lord that you're sorry you didn't know that He'd called you to be a king. You may feel a hand place a crown on your head. Ask Him to teach you how to be a king.

One thing that happens when you accept your mantle is that so much favor rests on you that people recognize it wherever you go. The atmosphere changes when you walk into a room. One of the best examples of this was a king of baseball named Ted Williams. Ted was the greatest hitter in the history of baseball. In 1941, his batting average was over .400, a feat nobody has accomplished since. He played for the Boston Red Sox for 21 seasons.

CHANGE AGENTS

There was a woman who for decades attended every home game that the Red Sox played. A lot of women love sports and attend games, but this woman never missed one. The most remarkable thing about her was that she was blind. A reporter interviewed her and said, "I don't want to insult you by asking this, but why do you go to every game when you're blind and can't even watch it?"

"I can feel the ballpark," she said. "I like the sounds, the smells, and the feel of excitement. When I listen to what's going on, I can imagine the game in my mind. But there's something I want to tell you. When Ted Williams stands up in the dugout, I know it."

She didn't say, "When Ted Williams hits a home run, I know it."

She didn't say, "When Ted Williams walks onto the field, I know it."

She didn't say, "When Ted Williams goes the plate, I know it."

When Ted Williams was sitting on the bench in the dugout, and he simply stood up, she knew it.

"How could you know when he stands up?" the reporter asked.

"When Ted Williams stands up, the whole atmosphere of the ballpark changes," she explained. "I can feel the change."

Ted Williams was the greatest hitter in baseball; he was a king of his field. He carried such a presence that it affected the entire atmosphere of the ballpark.

I could never be Ted Williams on the field, because God didn't give me his gift. However, I am a king in business, and if my hands are clean before the Lord, when I walk into a room any where in the world the atmosphere changes. There is nothing special about me. It happens because I am a conduit for God's power, and I carry His authority and favor.

He will do the same thing for you.

We are Change Agents for God. When we walk into a room, things change because God goes with us. It's that simple. The more you step into your destiny, the greater authority and power you will carry.

I'm not a woman so I can't speak for them, but I know that men need something to live for. We need something that we would be willing to die for. I think God created all of us—male and female—with a deep need for purpose in our lives. The more we step into the destiny that God designed us for, the more that purpose will be fulfilled.

If what you're doing with your life is possible without supernatural intervention from God, you haven't found your destiny. What God has called you to do is impossible apart from Him. As you step into God's plan, you'll start getting downloads as if on fiber optic cable from the Living God. God will give you supernatural knowledge, wisdom, and understanding that will cause you to win every battle.

BATTLE PLAN

When it comes to finding their destiny, most people are as lost as Dobie was. Like him, they've gotten stuck in life and don't know how to move forward. We were created by God to fulfill a purpose on earth, and nothing else in life will be as satisfying as walking out our destiny. The first and highest call in our lives is intimacy with God. From that place of intimacy, we will be crowned and given a mantle of authority to rule in the place where we are called. When we step into our destiny, we step into the miraculous. We step into a place where we will win every battle.

BATTLE PRINCIPLES:

- God is always willing to do His part. What takes the longest is for us to use the Bible like a mirror and discover who we are in Christ.

- We are called by God to be kings and priests.

- A kingdom is the king's domain, and God's kingdom cannot be limited to the brick and mortar walls of a church building. God's kingdom is all the earth, which includes the marketplace.

- The vast majority of miracles recorded in the New Testament occurred in the marketplace.

- The greatest shift in our paradigm may be learning to change our perception of ourselves.

- Each of us has a two-part destiny. The greatest thing you have been created and destined to do is to have an intimate relationship with God. That is the highest call in your life.

- The second part of your destiny is the rest of God's divine plan for your life.

- God is searching the world to find men and women who will accept their mantle as kings in the marketplace.

- We are Change Agents for God. When we walk into a room, things change because God goes with us. It's that simple. The more you step into your destiny, the greater authority and power you will carry.

- God created all of us—male and female—with a deep need for purpose in our lives.

- If what you're doing with your life is possible without supernatural intervention from God, you haven't found your destiny.

BATTLE STRATEGIES:

THE FIRST STEP: Our Highest Call

The highest call in our lives is intimacy with God. Knowing and fulfilling that call is the most important thing you can do with your life. It is from that place of intimacy that God will change your image of yourself.

THE SECOND STEP: Discover What God Created You to Do

How do you discover the second part of your destiny? You could do like I did when I screamed, "God, help me find my dog!" But you don't have to scream, because you have an intimate relationship with Him. First, you worship your way into His presence. Then you ask. God will answer. If you don't hear the answer right away, don't be discouraged. Keep listening. Keep seeking. Keep searching for God's heart. He will reveal it to you.

THE THIRD STEP: Fulfilling Our Priestly Duties

You may never be in the employ of a church, wear the mantle of a priest, and offer sacraments. But that doesn't mean you're not a priest. When you wake each morning and worship the Lord, giving Him the sacrifice of praise and offering to Him the sacrament of your life…you are a priest unto God. You are worshipping at His altar, whether it is the altar at a church or the altar of your heart.

THE FOURTH STEP: Crowned as Kings

A kingdom is the king's domain, and God's kingdom cannot be limited to the brick and mortar walls of a church building. God's kingdom is all the earth, which includes the marketplace. God has kings in banking, in construction, in agriculture, in government, in education, and in every arena of life. If you haven't been called to work in a church, you are called to work wherever God has planted you. For most of us, that means we are called, anointed, and appointed as kings and priests in the marketplace.

THE FIFTH STEP: Change Agents

We are Change Agents for God. When we walk into a room, things change because God goes with us. It's that simple. The more you step into your destiny, the greater authority and power you will carry.

THE SIXTH STEP: Miracles, Signs, and Wonders

You may be surprised to know that the vast majority of the miracles recorded in the New Testament occurred, not in the temple, but in the marketplace. As you walk out your destiny, be prepared to step into the miraculous. Be prepared to win every battle.

10

DIVINE PROTECTION

I looked out the window of the airplane as it made its final descent into Oklahoma City. Below me were patches of green, plowed fields of brown, lakes, and ponds. A thrill of excitement raced through me at the thought of being home. After flying all night, I'd just finished the last leg of my return flight from Israel. This trip had been a journey of faith for me, one that had changed my life forever. Just a few short months before, God had asked me to go to Israel. I had surrendered every atom of myself to Him, so I agreed to go. My business was new and struggling; although we had money for groceries and a roof over our heads, we were short on cash. If I had control of the reins of my life, I would have stayed home and worked a thousand times harder than I'd ever worked before.

Thank God, I'd given up control of my life.

I told God I would go to Israel no matter what, but I asked that the two lots we had listed for sale would be under contract before I went. Both were under contract. I also asked God to get me the

$200,000 I was owed. When I boarded the plane that morning, it hadn't happened. I had replayed the events in my mind hundreds of times.

The stewardess announced that the door would be closing in two minutes.

"God, that was the two-minute warning," I said. "I'm Yours, and I'm going to Israel no matter what. The rest is up to You."

I heard the door shut and felt the compression when it locked. The stewardess announced that all cell phones and electronic devices must be turned off. I pulled my cell phone out of my pocket, and a nanosecond before my finger pressed the OFF button...it rang.

The plane backed away from the terminal.

"Mike Galiga."

"Hi, Mike, it's Keith. Listen, I just wanted to let you know that we just made two $100,000 wire transfers into your account."

I had melted into my seat, in awe of God. Seconds later, He spoke to me.

THE HAND OF GOD

"Mike, it touched My heart that you agreed to go to Israel and pray for My people. Now I Am going to give you what you did not ask for. Satan is going to oppose you, and the easiest way for him to get to you is through your wife and son. I want you to know that I Myself will protect them. I will watch over them day and night. I want you to know that it will be My own hand that saves them."

I had flown to Israel resting in that assurance.

Now that I was almost home, I could hardly wait to see Dana and Michael, both of whom would be waiting for me at the airport. As the wheels of the airplane hit the tarmac, I turned on my cell phone. I had five messages from Dana. Unable to speak, in each of them she sobbed uncontrollably. My hand froze on my cell phone as I listened to her weep. Something horrible had happened, of that I was sure.

I noticed the strangest thing; my heart rate didn't increase. My palms didn't turn sweaty. Fear didn't sweep over me. My mind circled around one thought.

God promised to save them.

As the aircraft pulled into the gate, the voice of the stewardess once again came over the intercom. "Mike Galiga, where are you?"

I raised my hand. The stewardess continued in commanding tone. "Everyone stay seated! Mike Galiga, get up here!"

I grabbed my briefcase and started toward the front of the plane. Waiting for me was a huge Oklahoma City fireman, dressed in his helmet and bright yellow regalia. The expression on his face was as somber as death.

> "Mike, your wife and little boy were hit by a truck in the crosswalk in front of the airport," he said.

"Mike, your wife and little boy were hit by a truck in the crosswalk in front of the airport," he said. "They're in an ambulance on their way to Mercy Hospital. I have your wife's car keys. I know where she parked, and I'm going to take you to the car."

"Thank you," I said, following him.

THE PEACE OF GOD

It's hard for a man to give his family into anyone's care, even to God. Yet at that moment, knowing that I had surrendered them into His care, I'd never been so glad that I'd done anything in my life. *God, they're Yours.*

I waited for waves of fear and panic to knock me over, but there were none. I felt my heart beat slow and steady in my chest. My heart rate still hadn't sped up. When we reached the car, I thanked the fireman again before pulling away from the airport. My mind raced ahead during the drive to Mercy Hospital. What would I find?

Odd, that I felt so calm. I was at a new place with God. It was a deeper level of trust than I'd imagined possible. I jogged into the emergency room entrance and said, "I'm Mike Galiga. My family is here."

"Come with me, Mr. Galiga," I was told by a solemn nurse.

She led me into the bowels of the emergency room where I saw Dana, shaken but alive. My six-year-old son lay on an emergency table surrounded by doctors.

"Mike!" Dana said when she saw me. I held her while she shook. "It was drizzling this morning when we arrived at the airport," she explained. "As we walked across the crosswalk, I had the umbrella in my right hand. I held Michael's hand in my left. I saw an image of something coming toward me from the right, but it was too late to get out of the way. I felt a huge hand and arm throw me backward. It shoved me out of the way. The truck hit Michael and knocked him ten feet in the air. He landed on his feet looking right at the front bumper of the truck as it skidded to a stop."

> "I felt a huge hand and arm throw me backward. It shoved me out of the way."

After hours of testing, including an MRI, the emergency room doctor gave us his report on Michael. "I'm happy to tell you that your son is fine," he said. "None of us can figure out how a six-year-old child could be hit by a truck, thrown ten feet in the air, and have no injuries, but that sums it up. Your son doesn't have a scratch on his body."

Home never felt as sweet as it did when I ushered my family inside that day.

THE GOD OF MIRACLES

I was journaling a few days later when the Lord spoke to me. *Mike, because you prayed for My people—the descendants of Abraham, Isaac, and Jacob—and not for yourself, I promised to give you something that you hadn't asked for. I told you that I would protect you, your wife, and your son. It was My hand and My arm that saved them. I proved to you that I would keep My promise. Because you surrendered yourself to Me and you did what I asked you to do, I will keep My hand of protection over them."*

Love made me tremble. How could I ever give God anything that came close to showing Him the depth of my love? I'd already given Him all of me, my family, my business, and my money. I would have given them to Him a thousand times over if I'd been able. The more I poured out my love and worship to God, the more He poured out His blessings to me. I was outmatched. He loved me more; He gave me more.

That's the nature of the God I serve.

In reality my journey to Israel had started long before I boarded a plane for Tel Aviv. It started soon after I moved back to Oklahoma and started my own business. I was in Florida with little else on my mind than finally fulfilling my lifelong dream of obtaining my pilot's license. That's what I thought about as I drove through sun dappled land splashed with color. Without warning and from deep within the recesses of my soul, I began to weep. The words that came out of my mouth had been birthed in my spirit for they never passed through my mind. Sobbing, I heard myself say, "God, I want to get two million Jews home to Israel."

> The more I poured out my love and worship to God, the more He poured out His blessings to me. I was outmatched. He loved me more; He gave me more.

Thirty minutes later, I sat at my desk in Ground School, a paper and pencil before me. As I listened to the voice of the Living God, I grabbed the pencil and scrawled the date across the page before writing the words that echoed in my heart.

7/11/04

I will fully elevate you, Mike—now. Fall on your knees to me and prepare for My hand to come upon you as never before. I will use you to rescue My people for you moved My heart and I will awake. I love you, Mike. I love you.

I believe it was Jesus weeping through me for the descendants of Abraham. It was His voice that took hold with mine to ask for two millions Jews to be saved from death and returned to Israel. That, I realized, was my call and the reason God asked me to go to Israel. A few years later, I contacted the chief rabbi in the Ukraine. He flew from the Ukraine to meet with me in Washington, D.C.

> When the death angel swept over Egypt, killing the firstborn of every living thing, there was no death in Goshen where the Israelites lived.

"Why are we meeting?" he asked. "Why are you interested in this subject?"

"Rabbi, I believe in Jesus, and I believe that the Living God has shown me that the descendants of Abraham will experience 1939 Germany all over again."

Tears welled up in his eyes and streamed down his face. "It's already started," he wept. "In the Ukraine, I can't walk from my apartment to the synagogue without people throwing beer cans out of windows and screaming, 'Pig!'"

God will always call men and women to pray for and rescue the descendants of Abraham. That's the nature of the God I serve.

You don't have to read very far in the Bible to come across story after story of how God intervened on earth to save the lives of those who were in covenant with Him. The book of Exodus told how God had protected the Israelites from all the plagues of Egypt. When the death angel swept over Egypt, killing the firstborn of every living thing, there was no death in Goshen where the Israelites lived. God instructed Moses to have them use a hyssop branch to sprinkle the blood of a sacrificial lamb on the doorpost of their homes. That blood, which protected them from death, was a mere representation of the blood of Jesus, the Lamb that was sacrificed for the sins of the world.

When we face perilous times, how much more can we use our faith to sprinkle the blood on the doorposts of our hearts and our homes?

Exodus also tells how God parted the Red Sea, holding the rushing waters back while all the descendants of Abraham walked across on dry ground. When Pharaoh and his army chased them into the sea, the waters rolled back and drowned them. Most Westerners don't know the Israelites weren't owned by the Egyptians, but by Pharaoh himself. In order for them to be released from bondage, Pharaoh had to die. Thus, they received their freedom when he died in that watery grave.

> Sobbing, I heard myself say, "God, I want to get two million Jews home to Israel."

In the book of Second Kings, Israel cried out to God for help when the Syrian army attacked them. God blinded the eyes of the Syrians and routed them with horses and chariots of fire.

In First Samuel, God empowered a young boy to kill the giant that had terrified the entire Israeli army. In the book of Daniel, God joined three young Hebrew boys who were thrown into a fiery furnace. When they walked out unharmed, they didn't even smell like smoke. When Daniel was thrown into the lion's den for refusing to bow down and worship anyone but God, an angel muzzled the lion and kept him safe.

An angel broke Peter out of prison and led him to safety.

God delivered Paul from a shipwreck at sea, protected him when he was bitten by a venomous snake, and saved him from an assassination plot.

THE SECRET PLACE

That's just a partial list. The Bible is filled with stories of divine protection. It's also filled with scriptural promises of protection. Perhaps the most powerful of those is Psalm 91. This psalm explains how those three Hebrew boys could come out of a fiery furnace without smelling like smoke: They were safe inside the Secret Place of the Most High. It's that secret place where you're ushered into His presence each day. The key to unlocking divine protection is the same key that enabled you to live in covenant with God. You believed in your heart and confessed with your mouth.

In World War I, World War II, Vietnam, and Iraq, whole platoons of soldiers going into combat prayed the 91st Psalm every day and came out of the war without a single casualty. On the front lines of battle, they accessed the Secret Place of the Most High.

He who dwells in the shelter of the Most High will rest in the shadow of the Almighty. I will say of the Lord, "He is my refuge and my fortress, my God, in whom I trust." Surely he will save you from the fowler's snare and from the deadly pestilence. He will cover you with his feathers, and under his wings you will find refuge; his faithfulness will be your shield and rampart. You will not fear the terror of night, nor the arrow that flies by day, nor the pestilence that stalks in the darkness, nor the plague that destroys at midday. A thousand may fall at your side, ten thousand at your right hand, but it will not come near you. You will only observe with your eyes and see the punishment of the wicked.

If you make the Most High your dwelling—even the LORD, who is my refuge—then no harm will befall you, no disaster will come near your tent. For he will command his angels concerning you to guard you in all your ways; they will lift you up in their hands, so that you will not strike your foot against a stone. You will tread upon the lion and the cobra; you will trample the great lion and the serpent.

"Because he loves me," says the LORD, "I will rescue him; I will protect him, for he acknowledges my name. He will call upon me, and I will answer him; I will be with him in trouble, I will deliver him and honor him. With long life will I satisfy him and show him my salvation."

PSALM 91

SAY OF THE LORD

You just read it for yourself. There is a miracle in your mouth. Psalm 91 begins with the admonition to speak of God's protection. "I will say of the LORD, 'He is my refuge and my fortress, my God, in whom I trust.'"

After promising that you'll be protected from plagues and terror and every other evil thing, the psalm ends with two other things that God expects you to do. It says that if you love God and acknowledge His name, then you can call on Him and He will deliver you and honor you. What a promise! What a God we serve!

There's no question about it: we are living in perilous times. Yet, each of us has the privilege of starting each day in God's presence. We can live in the Secret Place of the Most High. From that place, you'll not only win every battle, you'll be protected during the war.

BATTLE PLAN

There's no point in denying that we're living in perilous times, but don't let that shake your confidence. God protected the heroes of faith in the Bible, and He protected my family. He'll do the same for yours. When you live in the Secret Place of the Most High, you'll not only win every battle, you'll be protected during the war.

BATTLE PRINCIPLES:

- The Bible is filled with stories of divine protection, and they're there for a reason: to boost your faith in God's ability to protect you.

- The sacrificial blood of an animal sprinkled on the doorposts of their homes protected the Israelites from the death angel. When you use your faith to sprinkle the blood of Jesus over the doorposts of your heart and your home, how much more will it protect you today?

- Whole platoons of soldiers going into war prayed Psalm 91 and never suffered a casualty.

- There is nothing to fear with God on your side.

- We each have access to the Secret Place of the Most High. In it is divine protection.

BATTLE STRATEGIES:

THE FIRST STEP: *The Secret Place*

Everything goes back to intimacy with God. It's from that place of intimacy that we learn to hear and recognize God's voice. It's also where we will discern His strategy against the enemy. When we step into His presence, we step into the Secret Place of the Most High.

THE SECOND STEP: *Pray for Protection*

Pray the 91st Psalm over yourself and your family on a regular basis. This will not only activate God's angels to protect you, it will boost your faith for protection.

THE THIRD STEP: *Say of the Lord*

There is a miracle in your mouth. When you are tempted to fear, say of the Lord, "You are my refuge, my fortress, and my God, in whom I trust."

THE FOURTH STEP: *The Blood*

Use your faith to pray the protective power of Jesus' blood over yourself and those you love.

A NEW PARADIGM

A s anyone can see, there is an order to the universe. Perhaps it's because I'm a lawyer and I understand man's laws that when I look around the galaxy, I recognize that there are higher laws than ours in operation. Some of them, like the law of gravity that governs earth, are easy to discern. Others, like the law ruling the creative power of our words, the law of surrender, or the law of forgiveness are less obvious. For those, we must delve into the Book of the Lawgiver.

As a boy, I designed a methodical way to search for my lost dog, Dobie. Likewise, I've spent much of my life searching out God's higher laws. In both instances, my search patterns failed; but God, recognizing my desire, revealed Dobie to me and then He began revealing His spiritual laws to me. That in itself is a spiritual law. The Bible states it this way: "Ask, and it shall be given to you; seek, and you shall find; knock, and it shall be opened to you. For everyone who asks receives, and he who seeks finds, and to him who knocks it shall be opened" (Matthew 7:7–8 NASB).

I like the way *The Message* version of the Bible says it.

> *Don't bargain with God. Be direct. Ask for what you need.*
> *This isn't a cat-and-mouse, hide-and-seek game we're in.*
> *If your child asks for bread, do you trick him with sawdust?*
> *If he asks for fish, do you scare him with a live snake on his*
> *plate? As bad as you are, you wouldn't think of such a*
> *thing. You're at least decent to your own children.*
> *So don't you think the God who conceived you in*
> *love will be even better?*
> MATTHEW 7:7–12

Whichever version of the Bible you read, the message is clear. If you search for God, He will find you. What you ask for, He will give you. If my journey to know the God of miracles was all about me, I wouldn't have bothered to write this book. I wrote it so that wherever you are on your journey, you will know that the best is still ahead. God is infinite, and that's why we will spend eternity with Him and never explore all the facets of His personality. I pray that this book sets you on course to experience the miraculous intervention of God in every area of your life. If it at least gave you a deeper hunger and thirst for God so that you ask, seek, knock, and find Him, then you have just embarked on the greatest adventure known to man.

Some people may say that the concept of invisible forces affecting our lives and businesses is nothing more than science fiction. I say that those people have not spent much time contemplating the complexities of our solar system, the waves of the sea, or the transformation of a caterpillar into a butterfly.

The galaxies of our universe are ever expanding, developing, and growing. That, I believe, is God's desire for each of us. He doesn't want us stuck somewhere like Dobie was, unable to move past the limitations of our own leashes. Like petroglyphs carved into ancient rock, the world around us is a canvas on which God has painted a story of love, loss, and restoration. From Adam all the way to you and me and to our descendents, it is a story of ordinary, finite lives that experience a divine intersection with the limitless love and power of God.

This much I know, the Living God is alive, closer than our next breath, and wooing each of us to awaken to His presence. To do so means that we must shift into a new paradigm; it's a paradigm where we wake each day to the wonder of being created in God's image. It's a paradigm that blasts away the limits of life as we've known it. It's a world filled with joy that explodes from intimacy with our Creator. Deep calls to deep, and nothing on earth can satisfy that longing for God that He created in us. It is a life marked by the supernatural.

It is a world where we will win every battle.

ENDNOTES

1 Mark Yarnell & Kevin B. McCommon, *Power Speaking: A Guide to Confidence & Career Growth*, USA Books, Evanston, New York, Miami, 1987, pp. 108, 109.

2 Linda Sharaby, "Israel's Economic Growth: Success Without Security," *MERIA* Journal, Volume 6, No. 3, September 2002.

3 The Zionist Youth, Israel—A Light to the Nations, Israel Facts, June 2003.

To contact Michael Galiga
for speaking, personal coaching,
and training, please call
Koechel Peterson & Associates
at 1-866-721-5017.

To order additional copies of this book,
call Bronze Bow Publishing toll free at
866.724.8200
or go to
www.bronzebowpublishing.com.